THE **COMPLETE IDIOT'S GUIDE**® TO

Staging Your Home to Sell

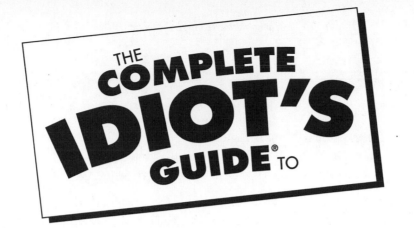

THE **COMPLETE IDIOT'S GUIDE**® TO

Staging Your Home to Sell

by Julie Dana and Marcia Layton Turner

ALPHA

A member of Penguin Group (USA) Inc.

To our families, who decorate our lives beautifully.

ALPHA BOOKS

Published by the Penguin Group

Penguin Group (USA) Inc., 375 Hudson Street, New York, New York 10014, U.S.A.

Penguin Group (Canada), 10 Alcorn Avenue, Toronto, Ontario, Canada M4V 3B2 (a division of Pearson Penguin Canada Inc.)

Penguin Books Ltd, 80 Strand, London WC2R 0RL, England

Penguin Ireland, 25 St Stephen's Green, Dublin 2, Ireland (a division of Penguin Books Ltd)

Penguin Group (Australia), 250 Camberwell Road, Camberwell, Victoria 3124, Australia (a division of Pearson Australia Group Pty Ltd)

Penguin Books India Pvt Ltd, 11 Community Centre, Panchsheel Park, New Delhi—110 017, India

Penguin Group (NZ), cnr Airborne and Rosedale Roads, Albany, Auckland 1310, New Zealand (a division of Pearson New Zealand Ltd)

Penguin Books (South Africa) (Pty) Ltd, 24 Sturdee Avenue, Rosebank, Johannesburg 2196, South Africa

Penguin Books Ltd, Registered Offices: 80 Strand, London WC2R 0RL, England

Copyright © 2007 by Julie Dana and Marcia Layton Turner

International Standard Book Number: 978-1-59257-611-1
Library of Congress Catalog Card Number: 2006932996

09 08 07   8 7 6 5 4 3 2

Interpretation of the printing code: The rightmost number of the first series of numbers is the year of the book's printing; the rightmost number of the second series of numbers is the number of the book's printing. For example, a printing code of 07-1 shows that the first printing occurred in 2007.

Printed in the United States of America

Note: This publication contains the opinions and ideas of its authors. It is intended to provide helpful and informative material on the subject matter covered. It is sold with the understanding that the authors and publisher are not engaged in rendering professional services in the book. If the reader requires personal assistance or advice, a competent professional should be consulted.

The authors and publisher specifically disclaim any responsibility for any liability, loss, or risk, personal or otherwise, which is incurred as a consequence, directly or indirectly, of the use and application of any of the contents of this book.

Most Alpha books are available at special quantity discounts for bulk purchases for sales promotions, premiums, fund-raising, or educational use. Special books, or book excerpts, can also be created to fit specific needs.

For details, write: Special Markets, Alpha Books, 375 Hudson Street, New York, NY 10014.

Publisher: *Marie Butler-Knight*
Editorial Director: *Mike Sanders*
Managing Editor: *Billy Fields*
Acquisitions Editor: *Tom Stevens*
Development Editor: *Nancy D. Lewis*
Senior Production Editor: *Janette Lynn*
Copy Editor: *Emily B. Garner*

Cartoonist: *Chris Eliopoulos*
Cover Designer: *Kurt Owens*
Book Designers: *Trina Wurst/Kurt Owens*
Indexer: *Heather McNeill*
Layout: *Brian Massey*
Proofreader: *Mary Hunt*

Contents at a Glance

Part 1:   **In the Beginning**   1

1   What Is Staging?   3

Staging is all about preparing your home for sale in such a way that it generates more interest, sells more quickly, and at a higher price.

2   Doing Your Homework   11

Studying your competition—other homes in your area— helps you decide what to change about your own home to make it more appealing than others on the market.

3   Setting Budgets and Priorities   23

Decide which projects will generate the most bang for your staging buck with help from us on prioritizing.

Part 2:   **Initial Steps**   33

4   To Declutter Is Divine   35

Learn how to add space to your home without adding on, just by clearing out daily clutter.

5   Clean Sweep   53

A guide to cleaning your home top to bottom, with recommendations on products and technique.

6   Remodeling Choices to Consider   63

Room-by-room advice regarding which repairs are must-dos and which are not, including suggestions on when to hire the pros.

7   Curb Appeal   83

Setting the stage for prospective buyers to be impressed, even before they walk through the front door.

Part 3:   **Room by Room**   **101**

8 Entrances and Exits   103

Buyers fall in love—or not—with your home in the entryway.

9 Living and Family Rooms   117

The living areas are the heart of your home and important spaces because of how much time is spent there. Staging works here to make them feel more spacious.

10 The Dining Room   131

Creating a separate eating area worthy of special holiday dinners is what staging the dining room is all about.

11 The Kitchen   143

An image of cleanliness and freshness is critical in the kitchen, which is a big factor in the decision to buy.

12 The Bedrooms   157

Spacious, relaxing, and elegant are the kinds of words you want to pop into buyers' minds when they see your bedrooms.

13 The Bathrooms   175

Buyers should feel as if they've stepped into a luxury spa instead of your bathroom if you've staged it properly.

14 The Closets   187

Your closets are a gauge of how much room for growth there is in your home.

15 The Home Office   201

In addition to being neat and organized, there are subtle cues you can send to communicate that your home office will help buyers be tremendously productive.

16 The Basement, Garage, and Attic   213

Flexibility is the watch word when it comes to these spaces, which are primarily used for storage.

Part 4:   The Finishing Touches   225

17 Staging the Exceptional Home   227
*Vacation homes, rental and investment properties, and
estate sales all call for a different approach from your standard single-family home.*

18 It's Show Time   239
*Making your home sparkle for open houses and by-
appointment tours will get people talking about it, and
encourage offers sooner rather than later, before someone
else snaps it up.*

Appendixes

A Glossary   253

B Staging Checklist   257

C Timeline Estimator   265

D Resources   269

Index   273

Contents

Part 1: In the Beginning   **1**

1 What Is Staging?   **3**

Why Stage? 3
    Gaining a Competitive Advantage 4
    Aiding Innate Buying Preferences 4
    More Than Common Sense 5
How It Makes a Difference...6
Why It Makes a Difference 6
Staging Statistics 7
When Do You Stage? 8
    Making the Best First Impression 8
    You Had Me At Hello 9
Keys to Doing It Yourself...9

2 Doing Your Homework   **11**

Know Your Price Point..12
    Get an Appraisal 12
    Amenities for the Money 13
    Style Impressions 14
Making Comparisons..15
    Are You Above or Below Standard 16
    Neighborhood Lifecycles 16
Assessing Your Home 17
    Your "Before" Pictures 17
    The Sniff Test 19
Styling Trends..20

3 Setting Budgets and Priorities   **23**

How Much to Spend 24
    Doing the Math 25
    Typical Scenarios 26
Which Rooms Are Money Makers 28

Part 2:   Initial Steps   33

4   To Declutter Is Divine   35

Do I Have To? 36
Why Oh Why? 38
   Gives You More Square Footage 38
   Shows Off Pretty Features While Reducing Distractions 38
   Allows the Buyers to Visualize Themselves Living There 39
   Hides Your Personal Issues 39
   Saves Time 40
What to Declutter 40
   Personal Papers 40
   Mementos and Gifts 41
   Repair Projects 42
   Is It a Clothes Rack or Fitness Equipment? 42
   Reading Material 42
   Toys and Playthings 43
   Redundant Furniture 43
   Plants and Floral Arrangements 43
   Medicines and Personal Care Items 44
   Fun Paraphernalia 44
   Seasonal Clothes 46
   Pets and Their Belongings 46
   Kitchen Confusion 47
   Garages 47
   Cleaning Supplies 47
   Outdoor Spaces Get Cluttered, Too 47
Techniques for Decluttering 48
   Set a Date and Keep It 48
   Set a Goal for Bags and Boxes 48
   Set a Goal for Packing for the Move 48
   One at a Time 49
   Reward Yourself for Your Efforts 49
   Sayings to Live (and Declutter) By 50
What to Do with the Clutter 50

5 Clean Sweep   **53**

A Clean House Is Half Sold 54

Clean from the Top Down 54

    Ceilings *55*

    Walls *56*

    Floors *57*

Room by Room 58

    Kitchens *58*

    Bathrooms *59*

    Pet Areas *60*

    Outside *60*

Nontoxic Cleaning Alternatives 61

6 Remodeling Choices to Consider   **63**

Making Major Changes 64

    What They Have That You Don't *64*

    Why You Need to Keep Up with the Joneses *66*

Take a Good Hard Look Under the Hood 67

    Inspectors Have Gadgets *67*

    Do-It-Yourself Inspection *68*

Airborne Safety Issues 68

    Smoke Detectors *69*

    Mold *69*

    Lead Paint *69*

    Asbestos *70*

    Radon *70*

    Other Hazards *70*

Mechanical System Check 70

    Keeping You Comfortable *71*

    Don't Fiddle with That Roof *71*

    Electric Avenue *72*

    If Water Runs Through It *72*

    Foundation Station *73*

Inside 73

    Kitchen *73*

    Bathrooms *77*

Floors 78

Basements 79

Additions and Add-on Rooms 79

Calling in the Pros 79

Architect 80

Bricklayers or Stone Masons 80

Carpenters 80

Carpet Installers 80

Concrete and Cement Workers 80

Contractor 80

Drywall Installers 81

Electrician 81

Hardwood Floor Specialists 81

HVAC Installers 81

Landscape Architect 81

Lawn and Yard Maintenance 81

Painters and Paper Hangers 82

Plumbers 82

Roofers 82

7 Curb Appeal   83

What Exactly Is Curb Appeal? 83

Driveways 85

Sidewalks 86

House Color 87

Trim and Accent Color 88

The Roof 89

Doors 89

All Hands On Deck 92

Pools and Water Features 92

Accessorize to Impress 93

What's Your Number? 93

Mailboxes 93

Welcome Mat 94

Adornments 94

Lighting 95

Pets 96

Landscaping 96

Part 3:   Room by Room   **101**

   8 The Entrances and Exits   **103**

       The First Interior Impression.................................. 103
          What They See... *104*
          Getting Through the Eye of the Needle..................... *104*
          Spend Money Here *105*
          Make Minor Repairs *106*
          Declutter and Clean....................................... *106*
          Foyer Arrangement and Style Choices *108*
          If You Don't Have a Foyer … *109*
       Room with a View.. 110
       Stairways and Hallways to Get You Places...................... 111
          Make It Functional and Clutter-Free....................... *111*
          Stylish Additions... *112*
       Exit, Staging, Right!... 114

   9 The Living and Family Rooms   **117**

       Minor Repairs 118
          Fireplace *118*
          Flooring.. *119*
          Paint *119*
       Declutter and Clean 120
       Furniture Placement 122
          Floor Space *123*
          Lighting *123*
       Staging with Style 125
          Decorating Tools *126*
          The New Decorating Approach............................... *128*

  10 The Dining Room   **131**

       Reclaim the Space 131
       Whipping It Into Shape.. 133
          Repairs... *133*
          Declutter and Clean....................................... *134*
          Arranging... *135*
          Brightening *136*

Stylish Eating 136
   Styling a China Cabinet 137
   Staging Secrets 138
If You Don't Have a Dining Room 140

11   The Kitchen   143

Minor Repairs 144
   Tiles 144
   Stove Hood 144
   Countertop 145
   Flooring 147
   Walls 147
   Lighting 148
Declutter and Clean 148
   Sink 149
   Refrigerator and Appliances 149
   Trashcan 151
   Countertops 151
   Hanging Rack and Tools 152
Adding Style 152
   To Be Purchased 153
   To Remove 153

12   The Bedrooms   157

Focus on Buyer's Goals, Not Yours....................................... 157
   Purpose of the Bedroom 158
   The Focal Point of the Bedroom 158
   Other Furniture 160
   Bedroom Staging Example 160
   Selling the Bedroom 161
Making Minor Repairs 162
Declutter and Clean 163
Making It Light and Spacious 165
   What's the Wattage? 165
   Make It Look Spacious 166
   Show Storage 167

Arrange the Bedrooms.. 167

Make It Stylish 170

Make the Bed 171

Room Accessories... 172

If You Don't Have Very Many Bedrooms.................... 173

13 The Bathrooms 175

Minor Repairs 176

Walls.. 176

Floors 177

Counter 177

Grout and Caulking 178

Fan 178

Clean and Declutter 179

Personal Equipment... 180

A Thorough Cleaning 181

Staging to Sell 181

Enlarging the Bathroom 181

The Spa Image 182

The Powder Room.. 186

14 The Closets 187

Show There Is Room to Grow 187

Match Closet and Purpose 188

Minor Repairs Worth Doing................................. 190

Play Up All the Space 191

Declutter 191

Clean... 192

Brighten 192

Staging Your Closet to Sell....................................... 193

The Kitchen Pantry 193

The Linen Closet 194

The Master Bedroom Closet 196

The Coat Closet 197

The Hall Closet.. 197

Creating the Illusion of Space 198

15 The Home Office **201**

Setting Up a Home Office 202
  Remember Its Purpose 202
  Creative Spaces 204
Declutter and Clean 204
  Computer "Décor" 204
  Closet Considerations 205
  Lighting Necessities 206
Furniture Arranging 206
Styling 208

16 The Basement, Garage, and Attic **213**

The Basement 214
  Unfinished Basement 214
  Finished Basement 215
  Declutter and Clean That Basement 215
  Removing Odors from Down Below 216
  Make It Bright and Spacious 216
  Establishing Living Zones 217
  Adding Style to Your Basement 218
The Garage or Carport 219
  Declutter and Clean That Garage 219
  Styling Your Garage 220
The Attic 220
The Laundry Area 222

Part 4: The Finishing Touches **225**

17 Staging the Exceptional Home **227**

Vacation Homes 228
  Clear Out and Clean Up 228
  Props Set the Stage 229
  Reeling in Renters 230
Rental Properties 231
  Do Your Homework 231

Who's Your Audience?..231

Decorate for Them 232

Estate Sale...233

Getting Into the Cycle 233

The Work to Be Done 233

A Flipped House...234

Vacant 235

Cheap Furniture Outlets 235

Basic Furniture Requirements.......................................235

Historic Home..237

18 It's Show Time   239

Photos Worth More Than 1,000 Words 239

Taking the "After" Photos 240

Return to the Scene of the Crime 240

Oh, the Places They'll Go 241

Taking Control 242

Secrets of Stunning Pictures 242

It's the Equipment 242

Wait for a Sunny Day 243

Open House Options 244

Four Types of Tours 245

Real Estate Professional Open House.............................246

Broker's Open House..246

Public Open House 246

By Appointment Tour 247

Game Time 247

The Nose Knows 247

Bring the Outside In...247

Lights On 248

Valuables 248

Furry Companions..249

Last Minute Prep Work..249

Parking 250

Your Ultimate Goal...251

Appendixes

A   Glossary   253

B   Staging Checklist   257

C   Timeline Estimator   265

D   Resources   269

    Index   273

Introduction

Selling your home is an exciting time and we hope to make it even more exciting by showing you step-by-step what you need to do to make buyers swoon with delight over your home. This process, called staging, is all about helping buyers envision their furniture, their belongings, and their family in your home, enjoying it to its fullest.

Although it isn't difficult, staging does take some planning, effort, and a few purchases to set the stage for a high-priced sale. Fortunately, you'll get all the guidance you need and more here. When done properly, staging helps sell homes faster and for more money—often over the original asking price.

Staging is so effective, in fact, that in some markets, such as California, Florida, and Washington, D.C., it is practically a requirement. Many real estate agents will only list a home if it has been staged because they know how much easier and more profitable the transaction will be if the investment—of time and a little money—has been made.

It's also fun. Staging is an opportunity to apply your creativity to persuading buyers to want your home. We hope you enjoy the process!

How This Book Is Organized

This book is presented in four parts:

Part 1, "In the Beginning," explains exactly what the term *staging* means for homeowners looking to sell their property for the most money possible. You'll learn about research tools for studying competing homes, when to begin staging, what you should consider spending on the staging process, and what sellers frequently earn in the way of a payoff from staging. You'll also receive some guidance in prioritizing all the areas of your home, depending on your budget, to avoid overspending.

Part 2, "Initial Steps," leads you through the basic processes of staging, including decluttering, cleaning, and interior and exterior repairs and upgrades. We'll provide before and after pictures of homes to show you what we mean by clean and clutter-free. And if you're worried about what you're going to do with all the stuff you have in your home, we have suggestions for what to do with it to get it out of the house.

Part 3, "Room by Room," is the section where you tackle each individual room in your home, decluttering, cleaning, arranging, and styling it to appeal to the vast majority of buyers who may be interested in your home. You'll hear tips for making the rooms seem more spacious and maintenance-free—two things buyers want most.

We'll also offer solutions for dealing with common issues that come up as well as resources for staging rooms just about any buyer would love to own.

Part 4, "The Finishing Touches," deals with preparing your home for buyers to see, whether the property is a single-family unit, vacation home, rental property, or bequest from a relative. You'll learn all about enticing buyers to come in and then wowing them with a well-staged space.

Things to Help You Out Along the Way

You will notice that throughout the chapters there are some special messages along the way.

def•i•ni•tion

Most of the words used in staging will probably be familiar to you, but we've highlighted some you may not have heard before to help you get the most money possible when your home sells.

Money Maker

These are tips and suggestions that can have a major impact on the value of your home. Many are low-cost or no-cost ways to boost the appeal of a particular room or feature.

Experts Explain

Staging can work wonders, but we don't want you to just take our word for it. We've included these secrets, suggestions, and success stories from staging professionals nationwide to inspire you.

Staging Snafu

To help you avoid any missteps or common pitfalls when it comes to readying your home, we've marked these tips as cautions.

Acknowledgments

Sharing our expertise on home staging requires not just intellectual knowledge about the subject, but real homes and real homeowners to make that knowledge authentic. We would like to personally thank all the homeowners and referring real estate agents who provided great examples and genuine experiences to share with you. The photos in this book are houses just like you may have—not perfect, but real homes that really needed to be sold.

A most deserving acknowledgment also goes to Barb Schwarz and her staff at StagedHomes.com. As the pioneer of the staging industry, Barb has shared her expertise and techniques through her staging accreditation classes. Many photos were graciously provided by Stagedhomes.com and were taken by Accredited Staging Professionals around the country.

Finally, our agent, Marilyn Allen, of the Allen O'Shea Literary Agency, and the fabulous team at Alpha Books, have our sincere thanks for their help and guidance. Of particular importance are Tom Stevens, who championed the project from the outset, and Nancy Lewis, our patient editor, who made our material even more helpful.

Special Thanks to the Technical Reviewer

The Complete Idiot's Guide to Staging Your Home to Sell was reviewed by an expert who double-checked the accuracy of what you'll learn here, to help us ensure that this book gives you everything you need to know about getting ready to sell your home. Special thanks are extended to Joanne Lenart-Weary, of One-Day Decorating.com. Joanne has enthusiastically trained one-day decorators and one-day stagers all across the country. This book would not be complete without her client examples and great photos from her alumni.

Trademarks

All terms mentioned in this book that are known to be or are suspected of being trademarks or service marks have been appropriately capitalized. Alpha Books and Penguin Group (USA) Inc. cannot attest to the accuracy of this information. Use of a term in this book should not be regarded as affecting the validity of any trademark or service mark.

Part 1

In the Beginning

Part 1 covers the basic questions you may have about preparing your home to sell—what it is, when you should stage, and why you should even bother. The answer is that taking the time to stage your home can payoff big financially.

In addition to learning what staging is, you'll hear about how to conduct staging research. Research in-hand, we'll help you prioritize and set budgets for the staging work to be done. You don't need to overhaul your home, but there will undoubtedly be some essential changes—we'll help you figure out what they are and what you can expect to spend.

Chapter 1

What Is Staging?

In This Chapter

- The staging and marketing connection
- Styling your home for success
- Taking those first steps
- First impressions are worth money

Home *staging* is a relatively new service designed to help prepare your home to sell while maximizing its appeal to potential buyers. By putting your home's best foot forward at the outset, it's very possible that it will sell more quickly and for more money than you would have received without taking the time to stage it.

Part decorating, part marketing, part psychology, staging highlights your home's best features while downplaying any weaknesses, and helps buyers envision how wonderful it would be to live there.

Why Stage?

Home staging as a phrase and a profession is more than 20 years old. However, successful realtors have been offering staging advice for as many years as homes have been sold. It may not have been called staging, but the bottom line was to make changes that improved the opportunity to sell the property.

def•i•ni•tion

Staging involves preparing your home to sell by accentuating its advantages and eliminating or reducing the perceived negatives. Results are often a quicker sale for more money than expected. The marketing aspects of staging include all the work done to persuade a buyer to make an offer, including promotional activities, listing materials, and how the home is presented.

The demand for staging has grown considerably in popularity as home prices have risen and sellers have sought ways to boost their property's appeal. Barb Schwarz, a former real estate agent and interior designer in Bellevue, Washington, coined the phrase "staging the home for sale" in 1985. Today, professionals can earn accreditation as Accredited Staging Professionals (ASP) and Master Accredited Staging Professionals (MASP) through her training. Such professionals are excellent resources for sellers, although we're going to share with you the basic guidelines for home staging that will allow you to do most, if not all, of it yourself if you want.

At its core, staging is about gaining a competitive edge—an advantage over the other homes in your area that will make buyers prefer yours to the others available.

Gaining a Competitive Advantage

Although frequently thought to be synonymous with interior decorating, staging is more marketing than anything else. Decorating plays a role in making your home's style appeal to more buyers, but marketing also shapes how buyers perceive your home and its many features.

Staging is about determining what your competition is and how you can beat it. Focusing on what will sell the home and then present it in its best light by decorating and styling in a way that will maximize those said features. The major difference when decorating to sell is to not hone into your own particular taste but to focus on the target market that will be attracted to your house. That said, some style choices sell better than others and we'll tell you where to look for cues regarding how your home should look.

Aiding Innate Buying Preferences

Keep in mind that while buyer tastes and preferences vary, there are some buying habits that rarely change—and are almost innate. All things being equal, buyers usually choose the home with the most space and amenities. It is simply a human characteristic to want the biggest and best for your money.

Think back to your childhood. When asked to choose a chocolate chip cookie from a plate full of them, which one are you going to look for? If you're like most kids, you'll go for the largest cookie with the most chocolate chips. Who wouldn't? All else being equal, why not choose the largest, richest option. The same is true of homes.

Sure, there may be minor details between several homes under consideration, but most people will always choose the home that they perceive to be the biggest. Note we didn't say that they'd choose the biggest, but the one perceived to be the biggest. And that's part of your opportunity with staging—to make your home appear to be as large as possible. A potential buyer wants to feel like they are getting the most space for their money. In return, the larger you can make the house feel, the more money you will probably receive from the sale of the house.

More Than Common Sense

The most common criticism we hear about staging is that it's common sense.

Much of what you're going to learn may sound perfectly obvious and you might have done it even without our recommending it. You might have. But with the reinforcement and encouragement here, you're much more likely to do all the things you know you probably should. Because although something may seem like common sense, such as making sure there are no dishes in the sink when a buyer is touring your home, you'd be surprised at how many sellers have them out. Or making sure your closet is neat as a pin, with towels and sheets crisply folded. These details sound obvious, but the reality is that few homeowners take the time to do it.

What some people call common sense is really objectivity—putting yourself in the shoes of the buyer and decorating for them.

Without staging, most people cannot see the possibilities a home holds for them. More than 80 percent of the population cannot visualize a home's potential unless it's staring them in the face; less than 20 percent can see beyond the clutter or the purple floral wallpaper to see the potential of the space.

By staging, you're increasing the potential buyers for your home by up to 80 percent, because you're doing all the work for them—they don't have to imagine your home at its best because you've already done that for them. Sold.

How It Makes a Difference

Staging is like preparing for an important job interview. Imagine that you're up for a job that will pay the equivalent of your home's asking price for one month's work. Given the great windfall that would likely yield for you, you would probably do all you could to make the best impression on your interviewer, such as:

- Getting a haircut and perhaps even a little color to add some density to your natural color, or to cover up some gray.

- Buying a new suit if your current one is more than two years old or it is showing its age. Even if the suit you own is stylish and in great shape, you could improve on it by having it dry-cleaned, to freshen it up.

- Buying new shoes, or having the ones you own polished.

- Taking a shower, brushing your teeth, and applying deodorant.

- Covering up an obvious tattoo.

- Taking off your baseball cap for the day.

In addition to helping you dress for success, we're also going to give you the questions the interviewer will ask and tell you the answers he or she wants to hear. This book will help you do your research so you have a solid understanding of the market and what the interviewer—potential buyer—wants to know about you.

Just like a successful job interview, staging can help you convince buyers that your home is the one for them.

Why It Makes a Difference

Like preparations for an important job interview, staging can improve your odds of landing a purchase offer for several reasons.

First, staging helps you remove your personality and taste from consideration. It is important to eliminate your family photos, collections, and clutter so buyers can imagine themselves living in your home. They need to imagine their own things in the space. Until they can picture themselves there, you won't have a sale, which is why we declutter and depersonalize.

Second, everyone wants an easy, carefree home. Time is so valuable that you don't want to send a message that it takes a great deal of work to keep the house looking fabulous. A potential buyer knows it will require work, just like their current home, but they don't want to be reminded of it by seeing cleaning supplies everywhere or laundry in process. This is why we clean and then hide all evidence of the cleaning process.

Third, buyers want to feel they got a good value for their money, which generally means more space. Because everyone wants a larger home, you need to make yours seem as spacious as possible, which is why we show how much additional storage and living space there is.

Finally, most buyers are looking to move up in size or style from their old home. They want more space and more status through their next purchase, which is why we accessorize with items that convey luxury and abundance.

Buyers have a general idea of what they're looking for in a home and staging will help you persuade them to consider yours. Staging and Redesign Trainer, JoAnne Lenart-Weary, states that buying a home is a combination of competition and seduction. So by understanding what other properties you are up against and then pushing the emotional buttons that will encourage someone to fall in love with your house, you will increase the opportunity to sell your house.

Staging Statistics

Home staging is changing the way that real estate is sold. In some areas, such as California, Florida, and Washington, D.C., some agents will not list homes until they have been staged, because the results are so dramatic. In areas where competition is strong and price appreciation great, staging has become virtually mandatory because without it some homes just won't sell, or it will take longer, or the sellers will get less for the property.

Savvy real estate agents are helping the cause, by recommending to homeowners that they stage their home before listing it, for better results. Some real estate companies even have full-time staging professionals on staff because it's so critical to the company's success.

Money Maker

With the popularity of real estate television shows on channels like HGTV, more buyers are aware of home staging and now expect to be impressed. Staging helps ensure you don't disappoint them.

Done right, staging can make an impressive difference in how quickly your home sells, as well as in the purchase price. According to StagedHomes.com, here are the results of a survey conducted in the last couple of years:

◆ The average increase in selling price for a staged home versus a nonstaged home is 6.9 percent.

◆ The average time on the market is 11 days for staged homes versus 22 days for nonstaged.

◆ Homes listed without staging took 163.7 days to sell. Homes listed and then staged took 13.7 days to sell, and homes that were staged first, then listed, took 8.9 days.

Interestingly, a real estate broker in California named Joy Valentine was somewhat skeptical of all the claims of higher prices and faster sales she was hearing about staging. So she did her own analysis of 2,772 properties sold in eight cities in California sold between March and September of 1999. What she found mirrors what StagedHomes.com reports:

> **Experts Explain**
>
> According to the National Association of Realtors, the average staging investment is between 1 and 3 percent of the home's asking price, which generates a return of 8 to 10 percent. However, spending more will not typically generate an equivalent increase—this is the best return ratio.

◆ The average number of days on the market for unstaged houses was 30.9.

◆ The average number of days on the market for staged houses was 13.9.

◆ The average difference in sale price over list price was 1.6 percent for unstaged houses.

◆ The average difference in sale price over list price for staged houses was 6.3 percent. On a $200,000 home, that's a difference of $9,000 profit.

When Do You Stage?

The best time to get started in staging your home is before you do anything else.

Making the Best First Impression

First impressions are important, whether you're dealing with buyers, real estate agents, or neighbors.

Before you contact a real estate agent, for example, because they will provide an estimate of your home's value based on what they see the first time they tour your home. If the tour is less impressive, the suggested selling price will be lower.

You'll also want to stage your home before any photos are taken, which often happens while the real estate agent is touring your home. You want your home to look absolutely spectacular in the photos buyers will be looking at, so don't allow any to be taken until your home is staged and looking its best. If you already have your property listed and decide to implement some of our staging techniques, make sure your realtor takes new photos and replaces the pre-staging photos.

You also want to finish staging before the "For Sale" sign goes on your lawn or in your window, which is likely to generate phone calls and requests for an appointment. If you're not ready, don't allow prospective buyers to wander through.

You Had Me At Hello

Part of the magic of staging involves creating an excitement or buzz around your home. You want anyone who has seen your home to come away totally impressed by the place and raving to their clients and friends about it. You want anything said about it to be complimentary, rather than focusing on negative aspects. The intent of most potential buyers is to look for flaws as a method to justify the lower bid they will offer. Staging can help decrease the opportunity to bid lower than asking price.

Your goal is to grab buyers as soon as they walk through the door and, as they see more of your home, to convince them that this is the place for them.

You can only do that if you've invested the time to prepare for the all-important tour, the all-important interview.

Money Maker

A National Association of Realtors survey found that the longer a home stays on the market, the further below list price it drops. Homes that sold in the first 4 weeks averaged 1 percent more than the list price; 4 to 12 weeks averaged 5 percent less; 13 to 24 weeks averaged 6.4 percent less than list price; and 24 weeks averaged more than 10 percent less than list price.

Keys to Doing It Yourself

With guidance from this book you will have the know-how to stage your home yourself. Whether you want to actually get down on your hands and knees to complete the task is up to you, however.

Before you get started, consider how much personal elbow grease you are willing to invest and how much you intend to delegate. This will help set your project budget and estimate a reasonable timeline for completion.

Once you've made a commitment to stage your home, set a deadline for completion. Staging work, like most any home improvement project, can drag on for weeks and months if you let it. Don't. Gain momentum by giving yourself a time limit, and then move ahead.

Experts Explain

Staging is not interior decorating. The purpose of interior decorating is to make the house meet the needs of the people who live there. Decorating emphasizes the owner's interests, values, and hobbies. Staging does not. Interior decorators use the same setting of a house and similar materials and resources as staging, but the end goals are very different.

Objectivity is critical here. Take a step back and look at your house through the eyes of a buyer, rather than as the owner who has a personal connection to the house. This is no longer your home, but a house for sale. Your home is waiting for you elsewhere.

Finally, once you list your home, be methodical and regimented about keeping your home in perfect shape for a tour at a moment's notice. It may be uncomfortable to live in a staged home because it's not always convenient, such as when you pack up many of your extra towels or hide your cat's litter box, but it definitely needs to be shown that way.

The Least You Need to Know

◆ Buyers will almost always choose a home with more space and amenities, all else being equal.

◆ Although some skeptics may argue that staging is common sense, it's actually about being objective—being able to see your home through the eyes of prospective buyers and making changes necessary to persuade them to purchase it.

◆ Research done on the value of staging consistently shows that staged homes sell faster and for more money than unstaged homes.

◆ Staging should be done before anything else—before calling a real estate agent for an appraisal, before taking photographs, and certainly before showing anyone else the property. If staging after your house has been on the market, insist on updating photos.

◆ Staging is like preparing for a huge job opportunity in which hundreds of thousands of dollars are at stake. To what lengths would you go to make yourself appealing to your prospective employer? Those are the same types of things you'll need to do to interest a buyer, with the same possible result—a huge payoff.

2

Doing Your Homework

In This Chapter

- Studying the competition
- Discovering your home's price point
- Determining what standard features are
- Learning what's on trend

Staging your home will certainly make it more appealing to buyers, but whether it will be more appealing than other homes in your area will depend on how well you've done your homework. How does your home stack up against the home for sale down the street or two blocks over? What will it take to make your home the favored property? What extra steps can you take to get an edge?

That's what this chapter is all about—gaining a competitive edge so you know what you need to do to make your home a comparative knock-out. Finding out where the competing homes are, what features they have, what kind of condition they're in, and what the asking prices are is the equivalent of stealing the other team's playbook. By knowing what they have and what they're asking, you can play up your home's positives to make it more attractive to house hunters.

If you do your homework well, you won't just get a good grade from buyers, you'll get thousands more in your pocket.

Know Your Price Point

Before you begin readying your home for sale, you should figure out first what it might be worth. Determining whether it's a $100,000 or $200,000 property, for instance, will be important as you make decisions about how much time and money to invest in staging it.

Certainly a real estate agent could give you a ballpark appraisal, but it's too early to involve an agent. You need to do some digging on your own.

Get an Appraisal

One of the quickest and easiest ways to figure out what your home is worth, approximately, is to use a website that has gathered such data already. Some of the top real estate appraisal websites are:

- www.homegain.com
- www.free-home-appraisal.com
- www.homeinsight.com
- www.valuemyhouse.com
- www.electronicappraiser.com

Most will request information about your home and then have a representative contact you to provide the results. Many are free but some do charge a fee, so read the fine print before clicking "Send."

Experts Explain

According to the National Association of Realtors, a typical buyer walks through 9 properties, looks for 8 weeks, and moves 12 miles from their previous residence when buying a new home.

You can also look at sites like www.realtor.com or a local realtor's site and find properties with comparable features in your area to get an idea of what similar properties list for.

Another way to gauge your home's value is to look at what homes in your neighborhood have sold for in the last couple of years. Your city or town clerk should have a record of real estate transfers that you can review to find nearby properties and the associated selling prices.

If that's not convenient, another approach is to look through back issues of your daily paper. Most local newspapers today report on home sales, although there is generally no information about the home's amenities—just the selling price. But that's a start.

Once you have a ballpark idea of your home's value, even within a range, you need to determine what buyers expect to get for that price.

Amenities for the Money

Although you may have been watching the local real estate market for a while, in anticipation of selling your home, you may have missed some recent sales. But often your neighbors have not.

Talk to your neighbors about homes that have sold to learn more about the sellers' experience. Try to find out:

- What was the original asking price?
- What did the home eventually sell for?
- What were the property taxes?
- How long was it on the market?
- Why did the sellers move?
- How old was the home?
- Had it been updated at all?
- How many bedrooms did it have?
- How many bathrooms?
- Did it have a fireplace?
- How nice was the kitchen?
- Did it have any hardwood floors?
- Were there any special upgrades, like a granite countertop in the kitchen or wine cooler?
- Was the basement finished?
- How large was the garage?
- How large was the back yard?

◆ Did it need much work?

◆ Who was the real estate agent?

Granted, you may not be able to get the answers to all of your questions from one conversation with the lady next door, but through a series of chats with friends nearby, you may be able to piece together the history and general assessment of homes that have recently changed hands to gauge how your home compares.

Style Impressions

One convenient place to check out the inside impression of homes is on the Internet. There are many websites in which you can look at your competition without leaving your comfy chair—many *multiple listing systems (MLS)* include 360-degree images of a home's interior, or a series of interior photos showing most of the rooms.

def•i•ni•tion

A **multiple listing system**, more commonly known as **MLS**, is the local database of real estate for sale within a geographic area. Generally speaking, only real estate agents can post or list properties on the system, but anyone can view the contents on the Internet.

The best place to start is on websites of larger regional real estate companies. There are several large nationwide real estate companies that have fabulous pictures of your competitors (other homes in your area). Try: Coldwell Banker at www.coldwellbanker.com or Century 21 at www.century21.com. As you look at these photos, ask yourself:

◆ Does this home give me the impression that it is up-to-date?

◆ Does it look like they have started to pack to move?

◆ Is their home better than mine?

As you're learning about recent home sales, you should also start to attend open houses in your area. Stop by to take note of the home and how it compares to yours. Pick up an information sheet that runs down the specifics of the property, including number of rooms, sizes, mechanical system age, special features, etc. You may want to refer to this information later, when you decide on your initial asking price.

Check out each room, noting the overall impression, what you would do differently, how much work it would be to make changes, and what others touring the home are commenting on.

Also use these visits to screen potential real estate agents. See which ones are knowledgeable, professional, helpful, as well as pushy, obnoxious, or disinterested. You'll be in a much better position to choose one to represent you after touring a few homes.

Where open houses are carefully planned down to the last detail, drop-in visits are not. So once you have made the rounds and seen most of the homes in your immediate area that are on the market, arrange with a real estate agent to see some homes—make some appointments to tour them. It's especially helpful to see homes last minute, when you'll get a true sense of what the home looks like on a daily basis.

Try to see all of the homes in your approximate price range—including a number that are slightly above what you think your home is worth. Seeing more expensive homes will help you determine what you need to do to compete at that price level. What will it take to push your home up into the next price range? Do you need another bedroom or could you update your kitchen cabinets and flooring and be comparable?

Remember when you are checking out these other homes to keep your mission in mind. You are doing research to sell your home—don't be a shopper just yet. Don't confuse your search for a new home, if you haven't yet found one, with your challenge to sell your home for the most money possible.

As you look at other homes, you may find yourself giving them nicknames, which is commonly done even by professional real estate agents. Homes that you have looked at during an open house, or even on the Internet, could be called "the teddybear house," "the cat-pee house," "ugly wallpaper house." Keep this concept in mind as you work on positioning and marketing your home. What do you think people will call it?

Making Comparisons

Studying homes in your area in your price range will give you a sense of what the standard is for your asking price. Let's say you think your home is worth approximately $299,000, based on what appraisals have indicated and your tours of other homes suggest. Now you need to figure out what the standards are for this level of home purchase. Do the other $299,000 homes have wall-to-wall carpeting, or do most have hardwoods? Do most have builder-grade cabinets, or custom kitchen cupboards? Are the basements generally unfinished, or have most been finished off and furnished? What do most of the rooms look like?

Are You Above or Below Standard

Whatever most of the homes at that price point have is considered the standard—what home buyers will expect other homes at that price to have as well. And you need to know what the standard is so you can compare your home to see where it is strong and where it is weak. Essentially, how is your home better than the standard and how is it worse? And where it is worse is where you'll want to focus most of your attention as you begin to stage and market it.

Neighborhood Lifecycles

As you learn more about current buyers' expectations, you'll also want to pay attention to who is moving into and out of your neighborhood. Are empty nesters looking to scale back and downsize? Are they growing families looking to step up into a larger home? Perhaps they are newlyweds buying their first home together.

It's useful to know who your likely buyer is so that you can stage your home to appeal to their buying needs, which are likely to vary based on their life stage. Empty nesters will probably be more interested in a home that is easy to maintain, updated, with room for guests. Families, on the other hand, are likely to want to see ample bedrooms for their brood, with entertaining space, maybe a finished basement where the kids can hang out, and room to expand. Newlyweds might want something in between—a home that isn't too big, but that has room for a future family.

Knowing the approximate age of buyers looking to move into your neighborhood will also help you decide how much updating you need to do and also how you will approach the decorating aspect of staging.

Experts Explain

"Sellers are often hesitant to spend money to fix up a home just to sell it. I always tell my sellers, "Pay now or pay later." Failure to make repairs and improvement will result in a lower selling price or in funds held in escrow at closing. By making the changes now, the seller can control the cost of the repairs and reap the benefits of a higher selling price."

—Nanette Catarinella, *Room Styles Interiors*

If your home hasn't had much updating in the past few years, that might be okay if older buyers will likely be moving in. However, it might be more difficult for younger buyers to envision living there if they're surrounded by wallpaper from an era before they were born—there may be nothing wrong with the wallpaper at all, but if they're not comfortable with it, you've lost a potential buyer. If you're selling to the younger buyer, it will be worth your while to remove all the wallpaper and invest in newer appliances to appeal to their style preferences.

Assessing Your Home

The next step in doing your homework is to objectively assess how your home stacks up against the competition. And the key word is objective. That means taking a step back and looking at your home through the eyes of a buyer.

Your "Before" Pictures

The best way to do this is to take several pictures of each room in your home. Either invest in a one-time-use camera or make space on your digital camera so you have enough shots to take four or five pictures per room, at different angles.

Start by going outside and taking a picture of your home from the curb, to see what buyers driving by would see. Then take another one from the driveway, moving closer and taking in the whole front yard. Then come inside and take a photo from the landing. Take some more views once you're inside—three or four shots into each room.

Take photos from several angles in the room.

(Courtesy of Eric Straith)

Move room to room, as a real estate agent and buyer would, capturing the picture of the room from the doorway and then more once you're inside. Take pictures inside closets, inside the pantry, and out in the backyard. Pretend you're a buyer and snap away.

Also take a shot from one room into another.

(Courtesy of Eric Straith)

Then have the film developed and leave them in the envelope for two to three days. Don't look at them right away.

If you have a digital camera, have prints made but don't look at them immediately. Set them aside and don't look at them for a few days, to get distance from what you just saw.

Then, after a few days, leave your home and go somewhere to review your pictures. It's very important that you not do this inside your home. Head to Starbucks or the library or work, while on your lunch break.

The reason this is so important is that photos don't lie—they will show you exactly what your home looks like to outsiders. But if you're sitting at home looking at the pictures of each room, you can look around and convince yourself that it doesn't really look as bad as the photos make it out to be. And you'd be fooling yourself, because it may actually be in need of some serious help.

The photos will help you get some distance and become objective about the changes that need to be made in order to convince a buyer to pay lots of money for it. But until you see that there is room for improvement, there is no reason to proceed.

Looking at pictures is extremely helpful, but there is one area where photos are useless and that is odors in the house.

The Sniff Test

The most difficult thing to be objective about, no matter how hard you try, is your home's smell. Every home has one, of course, but some are more potent than others and some are more objectionable.

The best way to assess what your home smells like, and then what you can do about it, is to ask a friend who doesn't come over much to visit. Ask them to be brutally honest about what they smell when they walk in the home. Explain that their honesty will help you make some changes that will lead to more money in your pocket. Then invite them in.

Remember that odors don't have to be strong to kill a sale. More people than you realize are extra sensitive to smells. Even the faintest odor can make a huge difference in the appeal of your house.

Some stagers and real estate agents make contracts with the owner that they will not smoke inside the house when it is on the market nor will they cook fish. These smells can linger for days.

Don't make the mistake of covering up the smells, take care of the source. You can read more about dealing with this issue in the next chapters.

Staging Snafu

In the past it was customary to put potpourri on the stove or brownies in the oven to add a home sweet home smell when buyers were touring the home. Today, however, with allergies more prevalent, you may get a different reaction than the one you were hoping for. A better option is to open your windows for ten minutes prior to a home tour for a clean and fresh smell.

Many homeowners skip this test and focus solely on furniture arrangement, cleaning, and accessorizing. And they miss out on a key factor in the home buying process. The fact is that no matter how gorgeous a home, if it has an unpleasant odor, it will be much harder to sell. A bad odor instantly gives a home a sense of not being as clean as it may be so it becomes a negative in two ways.

There are a number of sources of scents and odors, some of which you might not be aware:

◆ Smoking

◆ Animals/pets

- Ethnic cooking

- Incontinence

- Medicine, such as vaporizers or rubs

With a friend's help you can identify any odors, track down the source, and eliminate it, to make your home more attractive to buyers.

Once you have eliminated the bad odors, use subtle fragrances to make the property feel more desirable. However, it is never appropriate in today's world of full disclosure to mask odors such as mold or mildew.

Styling Trends

Most buyers want a home that is *on trend*. They generally don't want a home that is out of style, or outdated. The general guideline for being in or out of style is that if the decorating style in your home is more than 10 years old, it is outdated. Time flies, so most homeowners lose track of when updates actually happened. Although it may seem like last year that you painted the bathroom mauve, it's more likely that it's been 10 or 11 years, so it's time to paint.

def•i•ni•tion

On trend refers to a style that is current in fashion; it's up-to-date.

As you're doing your research to learn more about home sales in your area, you should also research what is considered *on trend*.

Knowing what is currently considered stylish in home décor will help you once you begin to rearrange and style your home to appeal to buyers. Sometimes being on trend is hard to explain, but you just know it when you see it. For instance, you can probably easily visualize a "little old lady" house. It would have dark, heavy drapes, lots of small tchotckes, and doilies on the tables. Decorating in a dated way will give the home the perception of being older than it is. This will carry over to the potential buyer's impression of the things they can not see, such as wiring, plumbing and more.

You may be wondering why being on trend is important. After all, you are selling your home, not your belongings, right? But staging your home and marketing it is a package. The style sets a tone for the home, which makes buyers desire it.

There are two reasons why you need to be on trend:

1. If the decorating message is up-to-date, people will assume the mechanics of the home are also up-to-date.

2. If the decorating message is fresh, buyers will associate it with good taste and increased status. If your home is just like their current one, why should they buy it? But if your home is fresh, up-to-date, and cool, they will want to buy it.

To find out what's on trend, look to decorating and women's magazines for tips. Try publications like:

- *Better Homes and Gardens*
- *Home*
- *InStyle Home*
- *Domino*

Staging Snafu

Don't give any of your rooms themes, such as lighthouses or a 1960s retro look. Such rooms only appeal to such a small segment of the population that you might reduce your chances of selling your home if you stick with a room theme anywhere.

All feature rooms with a streamlined, clean look and few mementos and accessories—what is current today. And since that's what buyers want, that's what you should aim to give them. Emulate the style of the rooms you see in such major magazines.

The style message to look for as you are reviewing magazines and catalogs is the color. You will probably be painting your spaces a soft neutral to sell, but what about the other colors? If you don't see much navy blue in the magazine layouts, for example, then you will want to remove your navy accent pillow from the couch. Opt instead for something in a color everyone is raving about in print.

Money Maker

Large accessories will give a room the perception of space as there is less "visual clutter" to slow the eye down. This will actually makes the space seem larger as the brain does not have to take time identifying the variety of objects in the room. When staging, you are selling the perception of space.

—JoAnne Lenart-Weary, One Day Decorating

Trends in accessories are also something to look for. Big accessories are more "in" than lots of small accessories. Think large vase instead of several little ones.

As you look at the magazine to see what is on trend, you may notice that furniture with a cascading or bustle back—also known as lumpy/bumpy—is no longer is style. Of course, the couch you are sitting on as you read this book may be just that style. So what should you do? Place a slip-cover over it while your home is on the market. Replacing it will help the house to show better and something to consider if you were planning on doing so when you moved to your new home.

Rearranging your furniture to focus on the elements of each room that will sell the house. Use room layouts in the magazines as a guide to the overall impression your rooms should make. At this stage, you might even consider hiring a stager or redesigner who is trained in this area. If using magazines for inspiration, don't try and follow them precisely. The idea is to create the general look and feel.

The Least You Need to Know

- Turn to websites to get an initial appraisal of what your home might sell for.

- Talk with neighbors and real estate agents to learn more about homes in your area that would be competing with yours on the market. Find out how your home stacks up—is it a good value for the money, or below average?

- To get an objective assessment of what your home looks like to buyers, take photos of each room and have them developed, but set them aside for a few days. Then open them away from home to see what visitors see.

- Study decorating magazines like *Better Homes and Gardens* and *Home* to learn what is currently stylish. Use these rooms for inspiration to model your rooms after the streamlined, clean looks the photos show.

- Ask a friend who doesn't spend much time at your home to give it a sniff test, telling you honestly of any odors they smell. Every home has a scent, but unless you get the help of someone who doesn't live in yours, you'll never know whether it's a deterrent to someone buying it.

Setting Budgets and Priorities

In This Chapter

- Sample staging success stories
- Using photographs to guide your work
- Which tasks are more than worth your time
- The benefit of a quick sale

You took the time to determine what your competition looks like and what the competition is. This has helped you to get an idea of what your home is approximately worth. It's time to start developing a budget and a schedule for the work to be done.

Breaking down the workload will help you decide which tasks you want to tackle yourself and which you'll need to delegate, given the desired time-line. Creating a ballpark budget will also help you prioritize projects in order to not break the bank.

How Much to Spend

Staging a home takes money. Granted, you can reduce your cash outlay by handling some of the work yourself, but some purchases can't be avoided and will require cold hard cash or a credit card. The good news is with a little creativity and imagination, some staging costs can be reduced or eliminated. The "common sense" elements of staging like decluttering and cleaning are minimal cost or free, but make a tremendous difference in how the home appeals to a buyer.

But the answer to how much you should expect to spend has no set answer. It all depends on the condition of your home and what needs work.

> **Experts Explain**
>
> Sixty-one percent of purchases are made by married couples, 21 percent by single women, 9 percent by single men, and 7 percent by unmarried couples, reports the National Association of Realtors.

Of course, there is a point of diminishing return—the point at which every $1 invested yields less than $1 in return—that should be considered. According to the National Association of Realtors, the best return on investment occurs when between 1 and 3 percent of the asking price is spent on staging. For that investment, between 8 and 10 percent return is typical, though certainly not guaranteed.

Now, when you read that, you may be thinking to yourself, that's a lot of cash out of my pocket. You're right, it is.

One of the psychological barriers to staging is that you need to spend cold hard cash up front, but the money you get in return is thousands of dollars in equity or at closing. But rest assured it's still money, and a lot of it.

Think of it this way, you spend $1,000 in preparing your home for sale. You think your house will be listed between $200,000 and $220,000. You would accept and be happy with an offer of $210,000 so you list your house at $215,000 knowing that most people offer slightly lower. Your house sells at the full asking price of $215,000. You spent $1,000 but in return you have gained $5,000 in equity.

The best part of staging is the creativity. As you read this chapter on budgets, don't think that you always need to spend a lot of money to get a good staging result. The fun part of staging is figuring out inexpensive solutions to cut the cost of preparing your home for sale. For example, you may not need to purchase new curtains for your living room windows. Actually removing the old window treatments will make the room brighter and more spacious feeling. This is exactly what you are trying to achieve. For no money, you made the space seem larger.

Be a bargain hunter as you are searching for items that add perceived value to the house. For example, perhaps you need new towels. If you can't afford to get thick luxurious ones costing $25 each, purchase cheaper versions at the local discount store but use them just for show and don't wash them.

Saving money by borrowing items is a great cheap solution, too. Do you need furniture on your deck to make it more inviting? Borrow a set from your sister across town for a week or two, or just borrow the set for the open house weekend.

Yes, be prepared to spend money for staging, but also think about alternative ways to trim money.

Doing the Math

That 1 to 3 percent investment equates to the following, depending on your home's value:

	1%	3%
$100k	$1,000	$3,000
$200k	$2,000	$6,000
$300k	$3,000	$9,000
$400k	$4,000	$12,000
$500k	$5,000	$15,000
$600k	$6,000	$18,000
$700k	$7,000	$21,000
$800k	$8,000	$24,000
$900k	$9,000	$27,000
$1 m	$10,000	$30,000

Keep in mind that the sooner you sell your home, the more likely you'll receive a value closer to your asking price—the longer it stays on the market, the lower the price typically drops. This means that an upfront investment may actually more than pay for itself because you won't have to drop the asking price later, or accept an offer that is far below what you were expecting.

If you list your house without staging, to "try and see what happens," and your home does not sell, you have just lost the "buzz" factor, which is difficult to regenerate. Remember the old saying, "you never get a second change to make a first impression"?

As a result, you may have to reduce your asking price. A typical price reduction is thousands of dollars and a wasted month on the market. If your home languishes on the market, you'll typically have to cut the price by at least $5,000 to $10,000. So you can invest the money upfront in staging or you can wait and see if you can sell it without staging, knowing that you may have to cut the price by an amount equal to or more than the cost of the staging. It's a risk either way, but you have more *up-side potential* with staging.

However you approach budgeting, you'll want to be realistic about what must be done (critical) and what would be nice to do (optional).

def•i•ni•tion

Up-side potential is the possibility that you will receive more than your asking price for your home. The opposite is the down-side, which is the risk you'll have to reduce the asking price in order for the home to sell.

Typical Scenarios

Sometimes it helps to hear how others approached the same situation, so we've gathered three case studies representing pretty typical sellers and listing what they spent on staging. As you read these illustrations, much of what is listed is what you would know to do anyway, and some you may wonder if it's really necessary. Making decisions about what to fix, what to remodel, and what to decorate with are key points of the rest of our book. These case studies will give you a little peek ahead to the next chapters, but keeping typical budgets in your mind is important to the end result of staging your home.

Under $1,000. Some homes with few renovations or upgrades will be fairly inexpensive and quick to stage. This home is a newly built condo that the Millers have lived in for three years. They recently had twins and realized recently that the Virginia condo is too small to meet the needs of their growing family.

Expenses:

◆ Repaint dark red living room to warm taupe	$60
◆ Comprehensive house cleaning	Free
◆ Purchase new shower curtain and towels	$55
◆ Purchase two additional lamps	$150
◆ Purchase odor machine (for diaper smell)	$250
◆ Accessories to emphasize vacation proximity	$50
◆ Rearrange furniture for traffic flow	Free

- Paint front door to stand out from adjacent condos $50
- Purchase stylish armoire to contain media clutter $200
- Total investment: $815
- Time required: One long weekend

Under $4,000. Other homes require more substantial upgrades and purchases, which boost the required investment. In this home, the Jones have spent 12 years in the house and raised their four children. They remodeled much of the house 10 years ago, but have not done much recently. Mr. Jones recently got an out-of-state transfer and they need to sell the house quickly.

Experts Explain

You can get your home ready for sale in a matter of weeks with proper planning, but don't rush it. See Appendix C for a handy time estimator.

Expenses:

- Rental of storage unit (packing up off-season clothes and kids' sports trophies) $500
- Declutter, toss, and give away   Free
- Replace dated kitchen appliances (will take with them at move) $2,500
- Give away big recliner to save space   Free
- Replace forest green kitchen counter with marble-looking laminate $650
- Strip wallpaper in master bedroom and paint over navy blue in son's room, strip wallpaper border in bathroom, paint (did work themselves) $110
- Move spare dining room chairs to back porch   Free
- Purchase new stylish rug and shower curtain for kids' bathroom $50
- Take down drapes in family room for more light   Free
- Steam clean carpets $125
- Total investment: $3,935
- Time required: Two weeks of daily work

Under $8,000. Some properties will need a significant amount of work to bring back their luster. In this case, Great Aunt Rita has collected quirky art and family mementos in her house for 40 years. She has done minimal maintenance and last updated her décor decades ago.

Expenses:

- Elderly dog urinated on carpeting. Carpet pulled up by family and professional refinished hardwood floors $1,000
- New rugs $100
- Painting of six rooms (outsourced) $1,200
- Replace dining room light fixture $200
- New mantel and fireplace screen $150
- Dishwasher and garbage disposal added to meet standard amenities in area $400
- Two new lamps $225
- Slipcovers to update old couches $300
- Replace kitchen floor with peel-stick tiles $200
- Replace concrete driveway and walkway $2,500
- Landscaping and lawn care $600
- Professional house cleaning $375
- Paint house trim $900
- Total cost: $8,150
- Estate sale proceeds to clear out clutter $347
- Investment required: ($8,150 – 347) $7,803
- Time required: Two months

Which Rooms Are Money Makers

After hearing about possible scenarios, it's time to get specific about what needs to be done at your place. To do that, you'll want to look at the photos you took of all the rooms in your home. Remember, the ones that showed you what buyers see when they walk in the door. It's time to look at them with a critical eye. As you review the photos, you'll want to give attention to the areas where you can make the biggest difference.

We're now going to arrange the photos in the following order:

1. ◆ Curb appeal
2. ◆ Kitchen
3. ◆ Bathrooms
4. ◆ Foyer/entryway
5. ◆ Living room
6. ◆ Dining room
7. ◆ Closets
8. ◆ Bedrooms
9. ◆ Office
10. ◆ Garage
11. ◆ Attic
12. ◆ Basement

As you probably know, some rooms are more important to the selling process than others. The two most important rooms are the kitchen and bathroom. Why? Because people know they cost the most to renovate and they use them each and every day, several times a day. If you have a limited budget, you'll want to address certain rooms before others. For example, if you can only replace the kitchen floor or the upstairs guest bedroom carpeting, you'll do the kitchen first.

Curb appeal should be your first focus. More than 76 percent of buyers do a drive-by first, either virtually or in person. This means they have checked out photos in the local real estate listings or online and have decided to proceed to take a look inside. If the outside photos are not appealing, then you will not get anyone in the door. You want buyers outside to say, "That house looks adorable, I've got to see inside." That's how curb appeal works.

To recap, when assessing the improvement and staging budget, the order of importance is curb appeal, kitchen, and then baths. Now continue to follow the preceding list to establish the order of importance. You may need to reorder the rooms slightly to match your floor plan, but follow your feet. The first rooms you see are higher on the priority list. In theory, by the time a potential buyer gets up to the last bedroom, they already love the home.

 Money Maker

To be sure your proposed timeline is reasonable, given all you need to accomplish, take a look at the staging Timeline Estimator in Appendix C for help in gauging how long your work will take. Also, the Staging Checklist in Appendix B can help to reassure you that you haven't forgotten anything major.

For example, in a recent house that was staged, the family needed to move quickly because of a job transfer and had limited time to get the house ready. They had two children. One bedroom that was downstairs was dark red. The other bedroom upstairs was dark blue. Yes, both should be painted, but the downstairs room is a higher priority because that's the room a buyer would see first, before the upstairs blue bedroom.

Some improvements are worth more than others, according to research done by HomeGain.com:

Improvement	Typical Cost	Increase in Sales Price	Average Return	Agents Who Recommend
Lighten and brighten	$86–110	$768–935	769%	84%
Clean & de-clutter	$305–339	$2,093–2,378	594%	91%
Fix plumbing, electrical	$338–381	$922–1,208	196%	63%
Landscape & trim	$432–506	$1,594–1,839	266%	72%
Staging	$212–1,089	$2,275–2,841	169%	76%
Kitchen/ bath upgrades	$1,546–2,120	$3,823–4,885	138%	83%
Repair flooring	$1,531–1,714	$2,267–2,589	50%	62%
Paint exterior walls	$2,188–2,381	$2,907–3,233	34%	57%
Replace carpeting	$2,602–2,765	$3,585–3,900	39%	65%

2003 HomeGain Survey of 2,000 real estate agents nationwide found that moderately priced home improvements, ranging from $80–2,800, made in preparation for sale actually yield the highest returns when a house is sold.

What's interesting about this HomeGain chart is they separate lighting and brightening the home, cleaning, decluttering, curb appeal, etc, from staging. For the purposes of our book, we consider this all to be part of staging. But this chart gives you a sense of how much value you're adding with each staging step.

You have looked through the photos multiple times and read the chart of most valuable updates. Now it is time to create a list—room by room—of the improvements needed. At this point you can make a list of things you are pretty sure need to be addressed, but just know that as you read the rest of the book, the list will probably grow. Some items may shift priority, but getting organized and ready for a list make the job get done.

You have your plan, it is time to delegate. For each upgrade, determine who will be responsible for completing it. Assign tasks to family members as well as outside services, especially if it requires a certain level of expertise.

Finally, set deadlines. Some activities need to be tackled in a certain order or the whole process will grind to a halt. Map out the various stages to try and keep the work on task. For instance, if you're making some changes to your kitchen, you'll first want to pull up the floor and redo the counters before you install appliances. Establishing the flow of the process will help reduce any lag time in between, so you can get your home on the market ASAP.

The Least You Need to Know

- Staging costs money, even if you do all the minor repair work yourself—there are accessories you'll need to purchase and materials that aren't free.

- A very basic guideline of what you should expect to spend on staging is 1 to 3 percent of your asking price, which frequently nets between an 8 and 10 percent return.

- Refer back to the photos you took of your home in Chapter 2 to help prioritize the staging process.

- Use the Staging Checklist (Appendix B) and Timeline Estimator (Appendix C) for help in scheduling the work to be done and estimating how long it will take before your home will be on the market.

- Research has shown that the longer your home is on the market, the further the ultimate purchase price drops below the asking price. This should be a major incentive to invest in staging upfront. The idea is to get it on the market and sell it quickly, for a higher price.

Part 2

Initial Steps

Like any properly organized project, knowing the order in which to accomplish the steps helps a great deal in completing it with as few head-aches as possible.

Decluttering, cleaning, and making necessary repairs inside and outside are essential for staging. We'll help you figure out exactly what you need to do and what you don't need to bother with.

We know it is sometimes difficult to know when to "spend money to make money," so we'll show you which repairs and upgrades will yield the biggest bang for your buck and reveal which aren't worth the trouble.

Chapter **4**

To Declutter Is Divine

In This Chapter

◆ The declutter–home sale connection

◆ Decluttering do's and don'ts

◆ Step-by-step tips for finding your counters and floors

◆ Dealing with detritus

Clutter is a home seller's enemy. It fills up space, makes your home appear messy and unkempt, and gets in the way of showcasing your home's best features. Clutter is the paper, the gadgets, the craft supplies, clothing, and mementos lying around the house that interfere with making a great first impression on buyers. All this is why decluttering is a very large slice of the staging pie.

When you finish with this slice you are well on your way to having your home ready for the real estate market. But until you declutter, you can't really attack all the cleaning, rearranging, renovating, repairing, or accessorizing that are all essential to the staging process. Yes, decluttering is a very necessary evil.

Keep in mind that staging your home to sell and living in your home are two very different processes. While a certain amount of clutter is almost required in order to function on a day-to-day basis, preparing your home to sell for the most money possible really requires that you create the impression that there is never a stray piece of paper or mislaid toy out of place. But since most of us live surrounded by lots of clutter, finding a place for it is one of the first staging tasks.

The biggest benefit of decluttering is that removing stray papers, paraphernalia, and junk lets a potential buyer really see your home. It also makes it much easier for them to start to envision themselves there. As a bonus, it helps you pack up early for your move to your new home.

So let's get started.

Do I Have To?

Before you begin, you need to adopt a purging mindset. Be ruthless about what you toss and look for opportunities to clear out the clutter. Imagine that everything you put away or remove will yield another dollar in your pocket, and then get to work.

Thorough purging of papers, kitchen accessories, clothing, books, tchotchkes, doo-dads, and anything broken can result in a dramatic difference in how your home looks. Just imagine how much more spacious your home will look and how much more money buyers will be willing to spend to own it.

It is important to note that when we talk about decluttering we're not expecting your home would be a serious candidate for TV shows like "Mission Organization" or "Clean Sweep." However, we do suspect that you have extra stuff lying around that can get in the way of a speedy home sale.

Coffee tables are often the 'catch-all' for everyday clutter.

(Courtesy of Julie Dana, the Home Stylist)

Of course, what you perceive as clutter and what buyers perceive as clutter may be two different things. Things don't have to be strewn about or messy to qualify as clutter, for example. It is the stuff of everyday life that we don't even see anymore, we're so used to it. But to a stranger, it is distracting.

A decluttered coffee table with simple accessories make the room appealing for buyers.

(Courtesy of Julie Dana, The Home Stylist)

Clutter is the pile of neatly stacked magazines in the corner that is partially blocking access to a cupboard. It is the pile of yesterday's mail you have yet to sort through that is sitting in the middle of the kitchen island. Clutter is even one too many end tables in your living room, making the room appear too full. Clutter is not garbage, but just too much of anything that makes the room appear busier than it could be.

> **Experts Explain**
>
> "The way you live in your home and the way you sell your house are two different things."
> —Barb Schwarz, founder of the Home Staging concept and President and CEO of StagedHomes.com

One of the essential tenets of decluttering is actually removing "stuff" from your home. There is some opportunity to file away important papers or hang clothing where it needs to be in the closet, but the vast majority of clutter really needs to be removed from the premises and discarded, donated, handed down, sold, or if absolutely necessary, moved to a storage unit.

Many of life's rules follow the 80/20 rule. Also called the Pareto Principle, the 80/20 rule states that 20 percent of something is generally responsible for 80 percent of the results. For instance, 20 percent of a company's workers complete 80 percent of the work, according to Pareto. It is the same at home with clutter. We only really use 20 percent of our belongings and the remaining 80 percent just takes up space.

Why Oh Why?

As you survey all the decluttering that needs to occur within your home, your enthusiasm may begin to wane. You may start to wonder if it's humanly possible to get rid of the stuff you'll need to. So let's look at all the amazing benefits you'll enjoy as part of this process.

Gives You More Square Footage

Potential buyers are looking for a home to buy, which means they are looking at rooms, and size and volume of the space. Clutter eats up space. Clutter makes rooms feel smaller. Clutter makes rooms feel cramped and dark. Clutter makes storage seem inadequate and closets woefully cramped. Decluttering—removing all extra stuff—actually adds space to a home. It is like building on an addition without the construction costs—cool, huh?!

Money Maker

Anyone in need of a quick and easy way to offload household clutter, without resorting to paying for a dumpster, should take a look at www.freecycle.org. Registered members post items they have to discard and other members can offer to take it off their hands, for free. The benefit for everyone is the amount of clutter kept out of landfills.

When you declutter, you show off the spaciousness and you make rooms feel bigger. Cutting back on contents makes rooms lighter, more comfortable. And—key point here—when buyers see that there is a lot of room in a home, they perceive that it is a good value. Depending on your current clutter volume, by sorting, decluttering, and packing, you can visually add the equivalent of 1,000 square feet to your home.

Shows Off Pretty Features While Reducing Distractions

Decluttering highlights your rooms' architectural features. Maybe you can't see the beautiful carved banister on the stairway because you have shoes on each step covering the details. Maybe you recently inherited a beautiful buffet table and the only space where it fit was in front of the largest picture window in the dining room. Which is okay, you think, because it gives you a place to stack all those magazines. Stop!

Distracted buyers don't see the home, they see your stuff. Instead of being interested in you, the current inhabitants of their potential home, you need to keep buyers focused on noticing the wonderful aspects of the home itself.

Allows the Buyers to Visualize Themselves Living There

Less clutter in the home helps buyers visualize themselves living there. This visualization is a critical step in the purchase process and will be discussed throughout the book.

When not up for sale, you want your home and your belongings to reflect your personality, to remind you of events or people, and to invite conversation among guests, among other things. That's what makes your home uniquely yours. But when you decide to put your home on the market, the role of your belongings change. Now, they need to support your goal of selling your home for the most money to the first buyer, not engage a buyer in conversation about your wife-carrying championship trophy or your stuffed cat Fluffy.

Remind yourself that you are selling a property, not your home sweet home, and not your favorite things. There is a difference.

 Staging Snafu

A sure clue that one of your personal collections has the potential to be distracting to buyers is that when your friends visit, they immediately want to see what you've added since they were last there. Don't let your pride of ownership distract you from your prime objective—selling your home for a pretty penny.

Staging is not about personal style choices but about marketing, and what sells homes. When you move into your new home, you can put your personal collections back up and allow the clutter to appear once again, but first you need to do all you can to sell your current home. To do that, you need to strip your home of your personality.

Hides Your Personal Issues

The last thing decluttering does is to remove evidence of any personal issues and attachments. Most clutter we collect is for personal reasons, however, buyers don't know that, nor do they really care. They don't care that those broken pots in the backyard came from your favorite aunt's house and she loved to garden and you just can't part with them—all they see are ugly broken pots cluttering the garden. Nor do they care that the floor-to-ceiling collection of artwork in the hallway was done by your son and you don't want to remove it.

Decluttering requires some level of detachment. Fortunately, looking at your home through a buyer's eyes can help you spot areas in need of improvement—decluttering, that is.

Saves Time

Decluttering saves time in another way, too, when cleaning and moving. If you have less stuff to clean around, cleaning will take less time. (Which is why in this book the declutter chapter is first and the clean chapter is next).

Cleaning is a breeze when you've invested the time in clearing off surfaces, such as counters, tables, and benches, and can see what actually needs to be cleaned. And the more you get rid of now, the less you'll have to pack and move to your new home.

What to Declutter

Sometimes seeing clutter is difficult when you live with it everyday, but buyers will spot it immediately. Here are some typical clutter culprits.

Personal Papers

Papers seem to multiply overnight, spreading out over all available horizontal surfaces without much provocation. There are catalogs, bills, school memos, social invitations, children's artwork, and more, coming in daily, with no end in sight. How do you decide what to keep and what to file or discard? Here are some suggestions to make the job more manageable.

A chart at the IRS website provides some general guidelines to help you sort through your paper clutter and determine which you can toss and which the IRS might want to see some day: www.irs.gov/publications/p552/index.html.

> **Experts Explain**
>
> "Electronic Labelers and paper shredders are 'must haves' for decluttering your home for sale and moving."
>
> —Linda Birkinbine of Keep It Organized, LLC

Other papers you may want to sort through and file or toss include:

- ◆ Children's artwork
- ◆ Coupons and special offers
- ◆ Paid bills
- ◆ School memos
- ◆ Calendars
- ◆ Catalogs and flyers

There is also the "Someday Pile." This clutter group includes the recipes you have clipped, but not put away. The stacks of photographs lying around waiting to be scrapbooked. The articles you have torn from magazines or newspapers but not filed. These items just add to the volume of the stuff we have in our homes. They take up space as well as time. These types of piles need to be dealt with immediately or packed away.

Then there is also the paper in the form of junk mail that's piling up, and the bills needing to be paid. All can be a big eyesore to people touring your home.

So try to pay your bills and then condense and reduce as much of the other paper-work as possible.

In the phone area, where scraps of paper have been known to multiply, ditch the yellowed menus from area restaurants and clean out the page markers hanging out of the phone book.

Mementos and Gifts

One of the most guilt-ridden issues to tackle is the sentimental things, such as family heirlooms, childhood artwork, and photographs, to name a few.

One approach is to let each family member have a certain number of boxes or a certain size box into which they can put treasures, but if it doesn't fit in the box, it gets handed down or tossed out. Another tactic, especially with larger pieces, is to take a picture of it, or of you with it.

Don't really love it? You don't have to keep it. Honestly, you don't have to keep it. Keep only the things that make you happy and that you truly love, and that goes for gifts and presents, too.

Money Maker

One of the easiest things to do to make your home more appealing to others is to remove your personal and family photographs. Buyers want to imagine their family living there, not yours. One or two discreet family photos are the most anyone should see.

Repair Projects

If you're like most of us, somewhere in your home lurks a pile of things needing repair. The torn pants you've been meaning to patch or the stereo system from college that just needs a new speaker wire fall into this category. Easy fixes you just need to get around to. Sure.

Today is the day you need to accept that these repairs will not be made. They won't be made because today you are going to throw these items away or give them to someone else who wants them. You haven't found time to finish—or even start—these projects, and with the work to be done on your new home, you certainly won't have time after the move. "When in doubt, throw it out" should become your motto.

Is It a Clothes Rack or Fitness Equipment?

Yes, clutter is the stationary bike in the bedroom or the treadmill down in the family room. Whether you honestly use it or not, fitness equipment can only be in a fitness room. If you don't have a fitness room, it has to be removed. Pack it up, loan it to your sister, sell it—your choice, just get it out of the space.

Reading Material

As any lover of books will tell you, the more the better, however, that is not the case when staging your home to sell. You want to show buyers that there is plenty of room to store their books, which will probably require that you clear some of yours out. So that bookcases don't look overburdened, you'll even want to remove some that are neatly shelved.

If you don't plan to have as many bookshelves in your new house, you can make some money selling your extras online at eBay or Amazon, for example, or by trading them in at a used bookstore. Libraries are always available to read any book or magazine you wish. You can also donate books to schools and libraries.

If you subscribe to the daily newspaper and get several magazines each month, you will be amazed at how uncluttered your home will look just by removing these piles of reading material.

The only exception to the recycling recommendation is a selection of a very few magazines to be used for style and marketing messages, which we'll talk about in Chapters 9 and 17.

Toys and Playthings

Staging your home for the real estate market and keeping it that way with children around is very difficult, but oh so necessary. The 80/20 rules applies here, too. The children will spend 80 percent of their time playing with 20 percent of the toys. One of the biggest clutter issues is stuffed animals. Pack them all away. One or two stuffed animals in a child's room are okay but more than that is clutter.

Redundant Furniture

You may not see extra furniture as clutter but if we go back to our definition of clutter, it is anything excess. Extra furniture is adding busy-ness to a room that is not needed, whether it is too many chairs in the dining room, or too many end tables in the living room. Extra furniture makes the room appear smaller and cramped, which is not what you want when trying to get the most money for your home.

In addition to furniture, there is such a thing as too many home décor accessories. Reduce clutter from little extras around your home, such as pillows, candles, potpourri, afghans, and throws. You want to make the décor in your home as neutral, yet inviting, as possible and too many little extras become distracting.

Money Maker

Now, there are important exceptions to the rules of decorating objects. You'll want to set aside a few select pieces to use later as props in staging your home to sell. These props may not even be your taste, but are needed to create a certain style for the general public. These include larger objects the size of a melon or basketball, such as large vases, large pretty bowls, large thicker candles, and decorative boxes.

Plants and Floral Arrangements

The only kind of plant you want in your home right now is a healthy, full, bushy plant. Any that are sickly, dying, or wimpy need to go because they send a warning to buyers. That warning is: "If they can't take care of a plant they probably did not take care of this home."

Staging Snafu

If your silk floral arrangements are more than two or three years old, it is time to throw them away. Dried arrangements must be tossed—no exceptions. Fresh equals new for buyers. Dried equals old and dusty. What do you want buyers to associate with your home?

A few select plants are acceptable but a nursery area and dedicated plant area is too much for many buyers. Give your plants to your gardening neighbor.

Medicines and Personal Care Items

Clutter can easily be found on bedroom dressers and bathroom counters because of the perfume bottles and moisturizers. There should not be any bottles of hygiene or grooming products out in the open at all. Period.

Although you may routinely leave out medicine in order to remind yourself or others to take it, when you're readying your home for sale, you'll need to remember to put it away. For one thing, you don't need to let strangers know what drugs you are taking and, consequently, the illness, diseases, or conditions you may have. For another, some drugs can be sold on the black market. You do not want to tempt unscrupulous people by showing them where they can steal drugs.

Medical equipment clutter, which you'll want to remove or store, includes special toilet adaptations, only occasionally used wheelchairs, oxygen tanks, and diabetic supplies. These supplies can make potential buyers very uncomfortable. Uncomfortable people do not buy homes.

Fun Paraphernalia

With hobbies, it is important to realize that not everyone enjoys the same hobby as you do. Hobbies include: professional sports team logos and equipment, art paints and easels, scrap booking supplies and paper, and model boats and cars, for example.

Just about all houses have a "junk" room, but when selling the clutter has to go.

(Courtesy of Nanette Catarinella, Room Styles Interiors)

With no clutter this back porch is charming and buyers will love it.

(Courtesy of Nanette Catarinella, Room Styles Interiors)

Buyers want to imagine their own hobbies and interests in this space, not yours. So pack it up. Crafters save clutter because they plan on using it someday. They think, "I am going to save these tiny scraps of wrapping paper for scrapbooking." Or "These broken tiles will be perfect for that mosaic table I want to make, once I find some more broken tile." Perhaps, but you don't have time for that now—you're moving.

Staging Snafu

Mounted animals of any kind, such as deer heads and stuffed ducks, do not belong in a staged home unless it is a hunting lodge. This includes bear skins or rugs. Take it down or risk losing a sale.

Piles of craft projects make it difficult for buyers to see how big the room is.

(Courtesy of Jennifer Keener of Amazing Transformations)

Clearing out hobby-related treasures transforms this room into a blank slate.

(Courtesy of Jennifer Keener of Amazing Transformations)

The solution? Take it to the curb. Give it away to the local preschool or nursing home. Offer it to your neighbor's kids. It must leave the premises. You want to sell your home don't you?

Seasonal Clothes

Nothing can help sell a home like loads of closet and storage space. Now is the perfect time to pack your off-season clothes up and anything you seldom wear, such as extra shoes, boots, coats, or flip flops and boogie boards, depending on your geography. Make room in those closets. We will review exactly how closets should look in Chapter 14.

Pets and Their Belongings

Fido and Fifi may be well-loved and spoiled, but their belongings are part of the clutter problem. And for buyers with allergies, the presence of pets could cause a severe reaction.

In Chapter 5, on cleaning, we will go in-depth on what you can do to eliminate pet odors and allergens, but for now focus on making your home look as if it doesn't have any four-legged occupants. This starts with putting the cages away out of sight, which does not mean in the kitchen or living room where they usually are. If this is absolutely not possible then you need to remember to remove them for each and every showing. Pet clutter also includes pet beds, toys, scratching posts, half chewed bones, and bulk containers of kibble.

Kitchen Confusion

One of the most valuable spaces in your home is the kitchen counter. It ranks right up there with closet space in terms of desirability. People value lots of counter room. And do you know what the average person does? Yes, they clutter the counter with appliances, canisters, bread machines, toaster ovens, crock pots, plastic containers of pasta, boxes of cereal, and the like.

Your job is to clear it off. Make the counter clutter-free. The maximum number of appliances or decorating elements a staged home can have on the counters is three, preferably fewer.

Garages

Chapter 16 is all about staging your garage, basement, and attic, including decluttering and cleaning it for buyers. The condition of your garage suggests to buyers how clean and organized your home is.

Cleaning Supplies

One thing we know about buyers is they want a carefree and easy home to live in. Translated, that means buyers do not want to be reminded that there is any housework that will need to be done. Ever. Even though you realize that no matter where you move housework has to happen, a reminder does not help the salability of the place.

Remove reminders of housework, such as dish drainers, laundry baskets, mops, and dirty sponges.

By the same token, piles of recyclables awaiting pick-up or drop-off need to be hidden away, too. Of course, recycling is good for the environment but unless it is exceptionally tidy and controlled, it is not good for selling homes. If this area is neatly contained and reduced to the current week's paper and plastic recyclables, you are probably okay. You do not want a buyer to see weeks' or months' worth of glass bottles heaped up in a pile. Now would be the time to get these things redeemed or carted away.

Outdoor Spaces Get Cluttered, Too

Do you have a sandbox but your children are teenagers? Do you have a rusty swing set? Be on the lookout for stacks of terracotta pots and plastic planting containers from the landscaping jobs.

Clutter you need to remove includes bicycles leaning against the garage, and balls or Frisbees lying around. Removing these items helps to show an immaculate home, but also prevents a potential buyer or real estate agent from tripping over something.

Techniques for Decluttering

After reading the list of clutter spots, you're now ready to tackle each area. Here are the specific steps you'll want to take to make your home clutter-free.

Set a Date and Keep It

One of the hardest parts about beginning decluttering is finding the time to do it. Yet the process is so critical that it will likely have the largest impact on the final value of your home. Think about that as you sort and sift through your stuff.

But rather than planning to take care of your whole home in a day, it is better to schedule time to thoroughly declutter a room, or maybe half your living space.

Write this date on your calendar and don't break the date. Think of it as a date that cannot be rescheduled. It may take a couple of dates to get the job done, but by setting a date you focus on the task.

Set a Goal for Bags and Boxes

Garbage bags must be the most useful and least expensive tool for sorting and decluttering. They come in several colors, which you can use to categorize what you've decluttered. Maybe use black bags for trash, green bags for items to sell, white bags for donation, and boxes for advance packing. Set a garbage bag and packed box goal for your house and keep going until you reach the goal.

Set a Goal for Packing for the Move

As you're sorting, boxing up, and getting rid of belongings in preparation for your move to a new home, create a timeline to help you methodically pack for the big day.

Perhaps give yourself two days per room in your home, during which you sift through and decide which stuff stays and which goes as you box it up for the movers. Or ask each member of the family to box up their own mementos and belongings in each room.

One at a Time

Don't get overwhelmed by thinking about your entire home—focus on one room at a time.

Start with the most difficult, most cluttered room so that any room after that will seem like a breeze. Have the colored garbage bags or boxes with you and systematically declutter. Review the specific clutter spots mentioned in this chapter to insure you go through it all.

After that room, take a breather and move on to the next. Steady and slow wins the race, but if you tackle your whole home at once, it is easy to get overwhelmed and basically create more of a mess. Sticking to the room-by-room plan will help.

Money Maker _____

The average household can take two to three garbage bags of clutter out of a home with barely a notice. However, the decluttering process for staging requires that you should be able to notice a difference. Making that kind of difference will take at least eight garbage bags.

Reward Yourself for Your Efforts

Sometimes we all need a little extra motivation to keep us going in large tasks. Setting up an intermediate reward can be a very helpful way to keep you moving. Setting up a large reward at the end of the project can work wonders, too.

Intermediate rewards could be as simple as a candy bar when you finish decluttering a closet. A larger reward could be going out to dinner when you finish sorting and decluttering the basement. Another reward could be based on the number of garbage bags you remove from your home. Establish a motivating reward for yourself to help keep you focused on the end goal—a beautiful uncluttered home to sell for top dollar.

Staging Snafu _____

Rewarding yourself with a shopping trip for material possessions defeats the purpose of readying your home for sale. So, rather than bringing in new clutter to be stowed, spend some time window shopping for your new home, during which you can keep an eye out for the perfect rug or lamp for your new space.

Sayings to Live (and Declutter) By

There are three sayings you may find helpful as you declutter:

◆ When in doubt throw it out. If you are having doubts about whether to toss something or keep it, fall back on this old standby and get rid of it.

◆ If you wore the fad the first time—you can't wear it the second. We all want to be young and hip, but in fashion, if you wore something trendy "back in the day," you are not of an appropriate age to wear it the second time around. It doesn't matter if leggings and a ripped sweatshirt (a lá Flashdance) are destined to come back in style—if you wore it when the style was originally popular, you can't wear it again without looking foolish. Give the leggings away.

◆ What goes out does not come back in. When decluttering your home, vow that everything brought out to be discarded or sold will not be brought back in if it does not sell. Make other arrangements to get rid of it.

What to Do with the Clutter

Now that you have amassed an amazing amount of clutter, here are several options for handling it.

Give It Away. Many local and national charities will come to take away your donations. Everything from business suits to yard tools to kitchen cabinets may be of interest to nonprofits, including women's shelters, Habitat for Humanity, or food pantries. A bonus is that you can receive a tax deduction for your clutter.

Throw It Away. Each bit of clutter that goes to the trash is one less thing you need to pack, and unpack in your new place. Check with your local municipality or trash hauler to learn if you need to make special arrangements to have larger items removed, such as furniture.

A service available in many parts of the country is a junk truck that comes to your home and hauls away anything you don't want. You often pay by the hour or by the volume. It's like renting a dumpster but much easier.

Put It Away. There will be some items you do not want to part with but hopefully you'll still be able to pack them away out of sight. Of your belongings that are left, the neater and more organized they are, the better your home will look. A few select packed boxes in a discreet corner of the basement or garage are okay and, in fact, sends the message to buyers that you are serious about moving.

Store It. Since the primary purpose of decluttering is making your home feel larger, removing much of the contents will achieve that goal. You may find that renting an off-site storage unit makes a lot of sense and reduces your stress about the process. You can pack up possessions you know you want to hold onto, but which need to come out of your home, and place them in a secure storage facility until you've moved into your new home and are ready to unpack.

Some companies, such as PODS, will even drop off a storage box into which you put your extra stuff, and will then come and take it away to storage. You don't have to worry about carting anything away yourself with this option, which is useful if you have larger pieces of furniture, for example.

Sell It. Items in good condition may be saleable, either by you or a retail business. The only caution here is that if the items do not sell, make arrangements so that they are not returned to you. Some popular ways to sell your cast-offs:

- Consignment shops
- Pawnshops
- eBay and other online auctions
- Amazon and Half.com
- Garage sales
- Flea market

Give the Stuff Back. As you are pulling your possessions out of the crevices of your place you may discover items that you have borrowed from neighbors and family members. No matter how long ago it was, now is the time to return them.

The Least You Need to Know

- Decluttering makes your home feel more spacious and more appealing to buyers, by allowing them to see more of the floors, walls, and windows.

- Aim to get rid of at least eight garbage bags of clutter from your home, if not more. Any less will not be noticeable and will make cleaning more difficult.

- Don't try and tackle your whole home at once; room-by-room is more realistic and less overwhelming.

- Anything personal, such as collections, photos, medical paraphernalia, and hobby stuff must be put out of sight or removed from the premises.

- Give it away, sell it, or toss it but it don't bring it back into your home.

Clean Sweep

In This Chapter

- ◆ Reasons to clean
- ◆ Step-by-step cleaning techniques
- ◆ Cleaning products you don't want to be without
- ◆ Nooks and crannies you might have forgotten

Now that you've removed much of the clutter of everyday life from your home, you can see what needs to be cleaned. Although your home is probably very clean already, we're going to show you some tips and tricks for getting rid of any remaining dirt, dust, film, pet hair, and odors, to make your home appealing to the majority of buyers.

The more you do to make your home spic and span, the more you're likely to make when you sell it. That's because buyers put a premium on cleanliness and convenience—the more you do to make your home appear easy to move into and easy to upkeep, the more people will be willing to consider buying it.

Experts Explain _____

"A bathroom can say a lot about a person. If it's clean and tidy, you wouldn't think twice about letting others see it. If it's not clean and tidy—or not as clean and tidy as you would like—it can also be extremely embarrassing."

—Linda Cobb, The Queen of Clean, author of Talking Dirty with the Queen of Clean

A Clean House Is Half Sold

In addition to making your home more attractive to potential buyers, there are a number of reasons for giving it your best cleaning effort:

- **To show pride of ownership.** A clean home suggests to buyers that your place is well cared for and will likely need fewer repairs or less maintenance.

- **To make people comfortable.** Some people are perfectly comfortable with a level of dirt and clutter and wouldn't be the least dismayed to find it in your home. But others can't stand it. To interest the largest percent of potential buyers, you'll want to appeal to the lowest common denominator—the level of cleanliness which most buyers are comfortable with—which means the dirt and clutter need to go.

- **To reduce allergens.** By reducing the amount of dust, dander, and mold in your home, you're reducing the chances that a potential buyer will have an allergy attack while touring, which improves the odds that they will be interested in your home.

- **To eliminate odors.** Every home has odors, but we're so used to them we don't smell them. But the more you clean, the more you reduce the source of any odors, which can be offensive to potential buyers.

- **To make the home feel more spacious.** Cleaning dust and film off the surfaces in your home makes them more reflective, which brightens rooms and makes them feel larger. Cleaning everything from windows to tables to pictures on the wall can help make a room sparkle.

Clean from the Top Down

When you begin to clean, you'll find it a lot easier to begin at the top, literally, and work your way down. That way, any dust and dirt from high places that lands on the ground will simply get swept or vacuumed away when you get to the floor level. Starting on the bottom and working your way up, from floor to ceiling, let's say, will only create more work for you.

Ceilings

You may need a step ladder to reach the highest place in your room—the ceiling. Start by using a feather duster or other dust magnet to clear away cobwebs around the edge of the room. Although it may not look like you have any cobwebs from the floor, when you get up close, you'll find all sorts of dusty ribbons waiting to be cleared away. And the corners are the worst!

Chandeliers are an area you'll want to dust first, then clean completely. With the chandelier lights off, to prevent you from getting burned, wipe down each lightbulb and crystal, to get rid of any dust and grime.

You'll be amazed at how much brighter the room looks with clean light bulbs in the chandelier, and how much more the unit sparkles.

Money Maker _____

In addition to a feather duster to remove dust, two other tools we've found quite handy, especially with tall ceilings, are an extension duster, which helps you reach higher than your arm can extend, and the Swiffer Duster. The more effective your dusting tool, the less effort you'll have to exert to get all those cobwebs down.

In rooms that have ceiling-mounted light fixtures, you'll need to unscrew and remove the glass fixture and wipe it off, getting rid of any dead bugs that have landed there, to get it clean. You may also find that using warm soap and water can really get the glass part clean, but only if there are no metal or electrical attachments.

Ceiling fans also need some attention. For best results, wipe down the top and bottom of each fan blade, removing any dust and dirt that has landed there. Turn on the fan and see if it is noisy when running. If so, then tighten up holdings to make sure it is operating as quietly as possible.

Money Maker _____

Here's a special technique for getting the best, streak-free shine on your windows. On the outside of the windowpanes, wipe them horizontally. And on the inside, wipe them vertically. It will be much easier to spot any streaks and to identify which side of the window needs attention.

Finally, any skylight windows should be carefully inspected, to confirm there are no leaks, and cleaned. Putting new caulking around the window isn't a bad idea, especially if it needs it, and the windows themselves should be washed inside and out.

Walls

Speaking of windows, as you move down from the ceiling to the walls, you'll want to wash all your windows inside and out, as well as the window sills and sash ledges. If you start by vacuuming the sill, you'll get most of the dirt up, and using warm soapy water to clean out the corners will give great results.

Money Maker

Doorways and trim in hallways tend to have more than their share of fingerprint marks, from people coming and going through the door. A product that we've found works wonders on these marks is the Mr. Clean Magic Eraser. Wet and use it gently on painted walls and wood trim to erase dirty finger marks in seconds.

You'll also need to take down any curtains, blinds, or drapes to give them a good cleaning, too. To clean fabric window treatments, such as curtains and drapes, follow the manufacturer's instructions for cleaning to protect and maintain the color. Some may require dry cleaning.

Blinds, however, can be cleaned using warm soapy water. The easiest way we've found to clean them is to swish them around in a bathtub, rather than attempt to clean each individual blind by hand. Once they're scrubbed, take them outside to dry in the sun, or lay them out on a plastic tarp or floor covering, to protect your hardwoods or carpeting from the water. There are also professional blind cleaning companies that will come right to your home and clean with a sonic system.

Don't forget your wall hangings such as picture frames, mirrors, and artwork, with or without a frame. Start by dusting them off and then spritzing any glass or mirrors with glass cleaner.

Check any and all woodwork around the house, including:

- Molding
- Crown molding
- Wainscoting
- Banisters
- Stairs
- Baseboards
- Door and window trim

Chapter 5: Clean Sweep   **57**

These all need to be dusted and cleaned—dusting alone won't bring out the shine. But don't use water on wood. Instead, try Liquid Gold or Murphy's Oil Soap, which will clean, shine, and protect the wood at the same time.

If you have a fireplace, you should clean out any ashes and add fresh logs or a cluster of candles. If the weather is warm, a vase of flowers is nice, too.

Furniture cleaning comes next. You'll want to vacuum all the upholstery and steam clean it using a steam cleaner you can rent from a local grocery or home improvement store. Take all the cushions off chairs and sofas in order to clean the top and bottom. Although you probably aren't selling your furniture with your home, freshening up your chairs and sofas will make them appear newer and will remove any lingering odors. What you are selling is atmosphere, and clean furniture suggests a well kept home. This will also help to eliminate lingering odors from smoke, dirt, and pets.

Wooden tables and chairs also need to be cleaned using Liquid Gold or Murphy's Oil Soap or Stickley Furniture polish. Wiping down bookcases is also important, since books attract a lot of dust.

Money Maker

If any of your furniture has small nicks or marks, invest in a product found at home improvement stores that effectively covers up any wood blemishes. The product is a magic marker filled with wood stain that allows you to touch up small spots quickly and easily.

Fabric that is on top of furniture, such as tablecloths, table runners, cushions on dining room chairs, and bedding, including mattress pads, pillows, sheets, and comforters need to be thoroughly washed. Many have allergens that cause odors in them; washing everything gets rid of both the allergens and the smell.

Floors

Either before or after you clean your furniture, you'll need to move it out of its current place on the floor. Now that you're working on cleaning the floor level, start by vacuuming, sweeping, and steam cleaning underneath sofas, chairs, and tables. Don't miss underneath pieces, such as beds. Be aware that most buyers will move furniture around to double-check whether it is covering up a big stain or spot on the floor.

Before you start cleaning the floor, however, wipe down the baseboards to remove any dirt and dust. If you do this now, you won't have to re-sweep or vacuum.

It's very important that you steam clean any carpeting, rather than thinking that vacuuming alone is good enough. In addition to brightening the carpets, by removing ground in dirt, steaming it also helps remove odors, which freshens your whole home.

Hardwoods should be swept and mopped.

Anything that's on the floor should also be cleaned, such as doormats. Better yet, if you have an outdoor doormat, replace it. Indoor rugs should be washed or cleaned according to the manufacturer's instructions.

While you're vacuuming, be sure and get the space in between the screen door and inside door, which can become full of leaves and dirt.

Room by Room

In addition to these basic cleaning tips, some rooms in your home have specific cleaning needs you'll want to be aware of.

Kitchens

The biggest item in the kitchen to focus on is the stove, because it gets the most grease and spilled food on it from regular use. To really make it grease and odor-free, you'll want to clean it inside and out. Of all the appliances in the kitchen, having a clean stove is the most important.

If you can, move the stove out, away from the wall, and clean behind and underneath it, which helps remove aging food drippings that also cause odors. Likewise, pull out the refrigerator and clean underneath it, too.

Money Maker

Ask a very good friend to tell you if your home smells. Ask them to be honest in order to help you. We all are so used to the smells in our homes that we can't often tell if it smells bad. But if a friend will help point out what your home smells like, or which rooms need the most attention, they'll be helping you immensely.

Clean the tops of tall appliances, like refrigerators, and cabinets, which are great dust collectors. Depending on your height, you may not be able to see the top of your refrigerator, for example, but a tall buyer may catch a glimpse of all the dust and grease and your positive first impression will be lost.

Your well-used countertops should be washed thoroughly, as well as anything sitting on top of the counter, such as baking canisters, toaster oven, or coffee maker, for example, which should all be wiped and cleaned. Even better, clean them and then put them away, out of sight, so as not to clutter the counters.

Believe it or not, it's also a good idea to clean inside kitchen cabinets and the refrigerator. You know buyers are going to look inside, so take a few minutes to wipe up any crumbs, clean any spills, and straighten the contents.

In your kitchen disposal, chop up a lemon and throw it in and grind it. It will do a great cleaning job and freshen the kitchen with a citrus scent.

Underneath your sink, clean up the cleaning products and stored items so that the space looks neat and smells nice. Buyers will look here and a neat and organized space will earn you bonus points.

Bathrooms

Another area where cleanliness is key for boosting a home's sale price is in the bathroom.

Around the sink and bathroom counter look for any stains and try to clean them up. Make sure they're decluttered and free of any grime.

Money Maker

As you move from room to room, wiping down surfaces using a sponge, use a new sponge in each room. Replacing the sponge frequently prevents germs and smells from being spread throughout the home.

If your shower or bath area has a shower curtain, it's a good idea to take it down and get a new one to freshen up the whole room. If you can't justify buying a new one, take it down and wash it to make sure it's free of soap scum and mold.

The same thing goes with any bath mats—it's a good idea to invest in a few new ones that coordinate with your new shower curtain, but, at a minimum, make sure they're clean.

Another item to replace is your toilet seat. Take a close look at the shape of your toilet before heading out to your local hardware store, to be sure you get one that lines up properly with the bowl. It's important to invest in a new one because (a) it's a fairly inexpensive upgrade and (b) older toilet seats just don't come totally clean, no matter how hard you scrub.

Inside the toilet bowl, be sure to get rid of any rust or hard water stains. Whink and Oxy-Flush are two products designed to remove rust stains that you might want to try.

Any tiles on your floor, around the sink, or in the shower or bath should be cleaned. A great tool for this is a Clorox Bleach Pen, which allows you to get into very tight spaces and brightens up older grout. If the grout is too far gone, however, you'll need to redo it. Yes, it's a mess, but regrouting has a major impact on the look of your bathroom and will be well worth it.

In all rooms, you'll want to empty trash cans and clean them out. The easiest way to accomplish this is to bring all your trash cans outside and hose them down with soap and water. Let them soak for a while to get rid of stubborn stains and smells. Just emptying them is not enough, however, because that won't get rid of odors.

Pet Areas

Pets are wonderful creatures, but some homebuyers may have issues with them. Whether they just don't like animals or are allergic to them, you don't want to have pets be the reason someone won't make an offer on your home. So you'll need to remove all evidence of them while your home is on the market.

With cats, you'll want to get a new litter box (the safest route) or dump out and completely clean the one you have to get rid of odors.

If you have a cage for your dog, you can clean it by washing the bedding and hosing down the cage.

If you added a pet door on one of your doors, and you kept the cut-out portion, you can pay to have it re-inserted for the buyer who may or may not have outdoor pets.

Money Maker

Pet stores have specific products for hard-to-remove pet odors. If you've found some areas in need of help, try one of these products.

With hamsters or other small animals, clean out the litter and wash the whole cage.

Smells are a big deterrent to a home sale, believe it or not. So depending on the situation in your home, you might also consider investing in or renting a sanitizing machine to get rid of any lingering smoke, pet, or kitchen odors.

Replacing the furnace air filter is also recommended, as well as having your air ducts professionally cleaned, which could be a selling point for anyone with allergies.

Outside

Although you've already washed your windows, it's a smart idea to wash the rest of your home's exterior. The fastest way to accomplish that job is to rent a power washer.

A few dollars spent on the rental can net you thousands of dollars in additional money from the sale—that's how big an impact a sparkling clean exterior can have on the price of your home.

Once you have the power washer, make good use of it by cleaning the exterior of the home, the porch, the lanai, and the driveway.

Staging Snafu

A power washer packs a powerful stream of water. If you use a power washer on siding with peeling paint, it may make the home look worse, by taking off even more paint.

Depending on the strength of the power washer, you may also be able to use it to clean off outdoor patio sets and outdoor furniture, as well as the grill—but check to be sure it's not too strong. Other outdoor things to be cleaned include screen houses and children's toys, such as playhouses, swing sets, and slides.

Nontoxic Cleaning Alternatives

We've already listed a number of products that we've found work wonders, but if you prefer nontoxic products, here are some alternative cleaning solutions:

- **Trash cans.** Sprinkle one half cup Borax in the base to cut down on mold and bacteria growth that can cause odors.

- **Linoleum cleaner.** First clean with soap and water and then mop with water and a capful of vinegar.

- **Hardwoods.** Rub in a thin coat of equal parts oil and vinegar.

- **Brick and tiles.** Scrub using one cup white vinegar in one gallon of warm water and then rinse with warm water.

- **Oven.** Scrub using baking soda and a slightly wet piece of steel wool, or try Arm & Hammer Oven Cleaner, which is reportedly nontoxic.

- **Tub and tile.** Wipe with vinegar and rub in baking soda with a damp sponge.

- **Windows.** Use a vinegar and water or lemon juice and water solution with newspaper to scrub.

The Least You Need to Know

◆ Before cleaning, finish decluttering so you can see what needs to be done.

◆ Start at the top—the ceiling—and work your way down to the walls and floors as you clean. This helps get rid of more dirt and reduces the need to go back over an area you just finished.

◆ Getting rid of dust and grime is important, but eliminating odors is even more essential.

◆ Using a powerwasher outside, to clean off aluminum siding, the driveway, and outdoor furniture can brighten the whole house and add thousands to its value.

◆ There are a number of nontoxic alternatives to popular commercial products which use vinegar, baking soda, and soap, for example, to achieve the same level of clean.

Chapter 6

Remodeling Choices to Consider

In This Chapter

- What is a major repair
- Address safety first
- Dealing with the outside
- Interior areas to repair or remodel
- When to call in the pros

Reviewing what large, and usually expensive, jobs need to be done before placing your home on the market may be daunting, but don't let it stop you. Establishing how much money to spend is an important decision and the overall project may impact greatly on the amount of money you may realize from the sale of your home. This chapter will give you an overview on areas that may need remodeling, and recommend who to call when the project is too big to tackle alone.

Although home staging does not generally tackle the subject of *major remodeling* and repairs, getting the most money for your home generally requires that you look at all aspects of the space, and identify what could be improved. There is no use staging a cute coffee table in the living room, for instance, if the roof is leaking on it. No matter how well the stage is set, the house won't sell if it needs serious repairs. We'll help you determine if you have any major remodeling or repair needs, and which improvements are worth making.

def•i•ni•tion

Major remodeling is structural and mechanical in nature, meaning that the shape or structure of the home may be changed, such as finishing the attic or revising the core systems, for example adding central air conditioning. Most of the time this type of work is accomplished by a licensed or trained professional (hint, hint).

Making Major Changes

Yes, major remodeling projects and repairs can be costly, but we'll help you decide which of those will yield a return on your investment—some repairs must be made, for example, but others may not be worth your time and money. To decide, you'll want to gather some information about other homes in your area, to see how yours stacks up.

Remember the homework you did checking out the competition in your neighborhood? This is where this knowledge comes in handy. What amenities do other homes in your price range offer? Is your house comparable? In this chapter, we are looking at specific upgrades and additions you might want to consider to make your home comparable to, or better yet, slightly better than your competition.

What They Have That You Don't

From your research, and maybe a neighborhood barbeque, you probably know if your neighbors have two or six bedrooms. You can also probably spot whether they have an attached garage or not, whether theirs is a walkout basement or not, and approximately how large their yard is. If you're in a high-rise apartment building, you can assess who has a balcony, which direction other units face, and, from the building floorplan, can probably find out how your place compares in square footage.

Before starting to make your list of remodeling projects worth the effort, you need to determine what your home is being compared to—what amenities or space do your neighbors have that you don't?

This home is attractive, but the front is nondescript—nothing stands out.

(Courtesy of Julie Dana, The Home Stylist)

Adding a new front porch and railing changes the entire look of the home, and gives it an advantage few of the neighbors have.

(Courtesy of Julie Dana, The Home Stylist)

Here are some typical comparisons buyers may be making between properties that you'll want to prepare for:

- Total square footage
- Recent repairs and upgrades
- Number of bedrooms

- ◆ Number of bathrooms
- ◆ Basement condition—finished?
- ◆ Front or back porch
- ◆ Garage car capacity
- ◆ Heating and air conditioning
- ◆ Utility cost

- ◆ Flooring—type and condition
- ◆ Kitchen appliance age and brand
- ◆ Window treatments—style and condition
- ◆ Back deck
- ◆ Landscaping

Of course, there are other considerations, too, and each buyer may have different priorities, but, in general, you'll want to compare your home to others nearby on these points to identify which areas need attention.

Why You Need to Keep Up with the Joneses

The bottom line is that your home needs to be comparable to other homes in your area to get an asking price that is in the same range. But your goal, and probably why you bought this book, is to make even more money for your home, right? By creating a home environment that is well above comparable properties, you're setting the stage to make more money—maybe even a lot more money—when you sell your home.

By tackling required maintenance and needed updates, you can control the cost of these major projects so as to get as much money for your home as possible, without pricing yourself out of the neighborhood.

When it comes to major structural or mechanical components of a home, such as a roof or septic tank or furnace, you have the option to make repairs yourself, before you put the property on the market, or to leave them for the buyers to deal with. Of course, the more you leave to be done by the buyers, the more leverage they have to knock your asking price down. Little by little, they can chip away at any profit margin you had, by arguing that the cost of such repairs should be deducted from the sale price.

The best way to prevent this situation is to take control and have the needed repairs done now, before the home goes up for sale. The less buyers have to complain about, the less negotiating power they have to try and bring the price down to account for any deficiencies.

A case-in-point is a friend who recently bought a new home and was able to negotiate the asking price down significantly because of major repairs needed that the former owners hadn't wanted to deal with. Instead of having the septic tank replaced, for instance, they had left it for the buyer to manage, which was fine, but in exchange, the buyer asked for, and received, a sizeable price reduction. Had the owner had the tank replaced prior to the sale, they would have been in a stronger negotiating position and might not have had to drop the price so much.

That's because the buyer expects a price drop equal to, or more than, the retail cost of the repair or upgrade. Yet if you, the seller, opt to have the repairs made before selling the home, you can look for a great sale, for instance, and end up spending less than the potential drop in price. To illustrate, let's say a new kitchen counter, to replace the stained lime green one from the 1960s, will cost around $8,000. If the home is sold as-is, the buyer will subtract $8,000 in his offer price to account for this needed change. However, if you go ahead and spend $4,000 to have it replaced on your own, you will save yourself at least $4,000.

Buyers will always estimate high, using pricey labor estimates and the most expensive quality product, but you can control the amount spent by contracting it out after doing comparison shopping and choosing a nice looking, but mid-range, countertop.

Of course, before starting any project, you will need to ask yourself if a few days of inconvenience will be worth the payoff in a higher asking price. Usually it is. We will get into what areas you will most likely need to remodel, or consider, in a moment.

Take a Good Hard Look Under the Hood

Now let's take a good hard look at the mechanical and structural characteristics of your home. You can hire a professional home inspector, or you can take a first run through yourself, if you have some background in real estate or property maintenance.

Inspectors Have Gadgets

Since the late 1980s, when states enacted disclosure laws requiring real estate owners to divulge potentially negative information about their home, it has become much more common, and often mandatory, to have a home inspection completed prior to the actual sale. That includes having a pre-sale inspection, so the current owner can be made aware of any issues that would come up during the buyer's home inspection and have the opportunity to correct them before putting the home on the market. As the owner, you don't want your dream deal to fall through because you did not know about the crack in the foundation or realize there was radon in the basement.

A professional home inspector will do a thorough inspection, which includes examining everything from the foundation to the roof and chimney. A home inspection looks at significant defects and common safety considerations, such as fire hazards and missing deck railings. If an issue is out of their scope of work, they will refer you to someone to handle these issues, or to get a second opinion from a person licensed in that area of concern.

The home inspection can then be used as a guide to address your home's major issues so you can be assured of getting the price you want for it.

Money Maker

Home Inspectors should belong to a national or state trade organization, such as the American Society of Home Inspectors or the National Association of Home Inspectors. Hiring one without such credentials may be a big waste of money, because there is no guarantee they know what to look for. Also, be sure to check with your local Better Business Bureau.

Do-It-Yourself Inspection

If you are a handy homeowner and a do-it-yourself type of person, chances are you know quite a bit about your own property. Depending on your skill level, you may be able to objectively assess which areas of your home could be remodeled or repaired to increase the value. You can also have a professional evaluate only those areas where you have less expertise.

A little later in this chapter, we will review these major areas. Please note that this information is for your general education and a more in-depth book or a trade professional may still need to be consulted.

Airborne Safety Issues

The most important thing to look at first is the safety of your home. This is a good idea no matter how long you have lived there, or how much longer you will be staying there—safety is critical.

Many states have minimum safety standards in some areas, such as requiring smoke detectors at certain locations within a home, or expecting that electrical systems are up to code. If safety issues are discovered, many states require that you tell the buyer about them.

Some safety issues can be corrected for as little as $10. Unfortunately, other deficiencies can be much more costly. But left unaddressed, your home will not sell for top dollar, if it even sells at all.

Smoke Detectors

All homes need working smoke detectors on each floor and near the bedrooms. Each municipality has its own laws, but common-sense suggests you should always have working detectors in your home, even if no one is living in it. This includes checking and replacing the batteries every year.

Staging Snafu _____

Don't be caught without a carbon monoxide detector in your home. Carbon monoxide is a colorless, odorless gas that can kill. Fortunately, carbon monoxide detectors are inexpensive, take no special skill to install, and are readily available at hardware and home stores.

Mold

Most household mold can be easily removed with a serious cleaning, but there are also more dangerous varieties that can make all who live in the home seriously ill. One particular variety of black mold can be especially hazardous.

If you have a mold problem, or even suspect you do, getting a mold specialist to take a look at it can save your family, as well as save your sale. A home with black mold but a cute-as-can-be family room, still won't sell.

Money Maker _____

There are several mold home-testing kits that, for under $10, can alert you to the incidence of black mold. Head to a home improvement store to get one if you'd like to do some initial tests on your own.

Lead Paint

Lead-based paint is one of the most common means of lead poisoning in children and is most commonly found in homes built or painted before 1978.

There are many local and state laws regarding requirements and disclosures about lead paint, which can get in the way of an easy home sale. An older property with chipping paint will have a difficult time selling due to both the unappealing appearance and the fear of lead poisoning. Check with your local real estate agent for requirements and referrals. You may only have to have a lead paint exclusion clause in your contract, but do your homework so it doesn't ruin your sale.

Asbestos

Asbestos is a carcinogenic product formerly used in the home in a number of places, including tiles and insulation. It can still be found, though usually only in older homes (prior to the 1980s), appearing as "cottage cheese ceilings," or kitchen tiles, or installation wrapped around pipes and siding.

The good news is that if the material containing asbestos is intact, you probably won't have any problems. But if you decide to have it removed, it is so dangerous that you'll want to hire licensed asbestos abatement contractors to handle the job. Do not try this yourself!

Radon

Radon is an invisible and odorless gas that can be found in areas all across the country, although not everywhere. It seeps up from the ground and usually enters your property through the foundation or basement and has been linked to lung cancer.

If radon is in your area, you should have your home tested by a home inspector or you, the homeowner, can also do the test. Be sure to follow the directions, however, to ensure your results are accurate. The test results will indicate whether you need a radon mitigation system to continuously pump out the gas. Do-it-yourself testing kits can be found at most home improvement stores for around $15, although having a professional test conducted is more accurate.

Other Hazards

Depending on where you live, you may not have radon, but you could have termites or carpenter ants or wood beetles, or the more unusual formaldehyde or electromagnetic fields.

Be safe and have all potential hazards identified and eradicated before putting your home up for sale. You want your place to sell fast, for the most money, without any hassles or lawsuits.

Mechanical System Check

Unless you are going to advertise your home as a "fixer-upper" or "handyman's special" (translation: cheap), you'll want to make sure the major mechanical elements are working properly. Top dollar returns on the sale of your house will be impacted negatively if these systems don't work. The behind the scenes aspects of the home aren't really sexy, nor are they generally visible, but they can seriously affect the selling price of your home.

With major system issues it is usually best to have a professional fix, repair, or replace the elements. Amateurs working with electricity or climbing a three-story roof can be extremely hazardous. Many municipalities require that mechanical system work be completed by a licensed professional—not using the services of a pro can cause delays because the local code officer will not grant approval.

Keeping You Comfortable

The relative importance of the furnace and the air conditioning unit in your home depends on your geography. A home without central air conditioning in Florida will stay on the market a while, but in North Dakota, a home without central air may be typical, since there are few scorching days of summer.

The bottom line with both heating and cooling is that they must work. Either have them repaired or replaced, but make sure they are functioning properly before selling the home.

And if you replace them, do not purchase the cheapest, most inefficient appliance you can. Get a modestly priced, middle-of-the-road furnace or air conditioning system so the home inspector and potential buyers don't have to wonder what other major appliances you chose to scrimp on. Being cheap with important systems may ultimately cost you in the sales negotiation.

Don't Fiddle with That Roof

You can't sell a home with buckets strategically positioned on the floor to catch the rain and expect to get a decent price—you know that, of course. But what if it leaks only when the wind blows a certain way? Do you fix it or get a whole new roof?

You fix it. Then you make sure you fix or repair any damage done by the leak. Although it may be tempting to paint over an old water spot without fixing the intermittent cause, professional home inspectors are trained to look for that trick. Be prepared to answer questions on how and when it was fixed and to provide paperwork to document the work. Again, roof repair is almost always better left to the professionals.

While you are checking out the roof, it is a good idea to check your gutters. They often get clogged and can cause standing water near your foundation. Gutters play such a large role in keeping water away from the house that some mortgage companies and house insurance companies may not give you a policy if gutters are not present.

Electric Avenue

Although newer homes must be inspected to receive a certificate of occupancy, homes more than five years old may be due for an electrical check-up.

And if you have noticed any problems, such as flickering of lights or frequent blown fuses, you'll definitely want a professional inspection to make sure you aren't in danger of overloading your electrical system. Not only is this dangerous for the buyers, it is dangerous for you while you're still living there.

Other indications that your electrical service may be a candidate for replacement prior to selling:

> **Experts Explain**
>
> According to the United States Product Safety Commission, aluminum wiring, once used to save building costs years ago, is a frequent cause of residential fires. It requires specially-designed switches, outlets, and insulation to be safe; it is usually recommended that your whole system be replaced.

- Your home is more than 40 years old.

- You have added more than one room to the house.

- Your house has aluminum wiring.

- You have an above-average amount of high-tech or high-electricity consuming appliances, such as a hot tub.

- You still have a fuse box, not a breaker system.

If you fit any of these descriptions, consider getting your electricity upgraded for a faster sale.

If Water Runs Through It

The decision whether to replace a water heater is an easy one—you have to have a heater and it needs to work and be leak-free. If your current one does not meet those two conditions, you'll want to start shopping for one that does.

Plumbing also needs to be in good working order. That includes the seldom-used toilet in the basement, or the outdoor shower used after days at the beach. If you have nonworking plumbing it makes buyers wonder what else does not work, and what else you have ignored. If these issues need to be addressed, contact a professional plumber.

Foundation Station

No matter what type of foundation you have, if it needs to be repaired, it can cost lots of money. If the property has major foundation problems, it also affects the structural integrity of the rest of the home.

Don't panic about tiny cracks—most often they are just part of natural settling—but the only way to know for sure that your foundation is intact is to hire a professional to examine it and address any needed repairs.

Inside

To get the most money for your home, go inside and take a look around. Some rooms may need to be totally remodeled while others may have minor repairs here and there to update them. Here are some of the most important projects to consider in each room.

Staging Snafu

According to the National Association of Realtors, the least likely remodeling projects to be undertaken are in-law suites, media rooms, exercise rooms, and utility rooms. You may want to use this as a reverse priority list for yourself and put any of these rooms at the bottom of your own list.

Kitchen

Kitchens today are a new status symbol. They are bigger and fancier in order to accommodate family and friends who casually gather there. It's no longer just a place to cook your meals, it's now a space for entertaining—and an important one at that. Potential buyers will use your kitchen as a "make or break" feature when comparing different properties.

A kitchen can eat up even a generous budget very quickly, so you'll want to carefully pick and choose where you invest your remodeling funds. The good news is that today you can find high-end-looking components in a moderate price range. For example, if you cannot afford to have a granite countertop, you can choose a new counter laminate, which looks remarkably like the real thing at a fraction of the cost. When remodeling or replacing kitchen parts, make it look as high-end as you can, while keeping the cost reasonable—you don't want to overspend and not recoup your investment when you sell the home.

Here are some guidelines to follow to help freshen your kitchen without breaking the bank.

Counters. One of the first kitchen elements to consider changing is the countertop. They are the most noticeable and, thanks to style trends, can show their age the fastest (meaning that even if you replaced the counters ten years ago, you may need to again in order to make them look fresh and updated). This is an important place again to think of the competition. What do other homes in your price range have on their counters? When choosing new counters, pick medium tones of a neutral color, such as beige. Warm tones traditionally sell better as they complement the colors of most cabinetry. Look for something that looks expensive but is really not. Ask salespeople at the local home improvement store what they are a selling a lot of right now. This is not the time to be too trendy and install passion purple counters because it is a close-out special; go with what will appeal to the largest group of buyers (and trust us, it isn't passion purple).

Cabinets. These can be expensive to replace, so suggesting you spring for new ones is not on our list of recommendations. The key is the selling price of your home. The expectation of a potential buyer looking at a $175,000 house is far different from someone contemplating the purchase of a $1,000,000 house. A good cleaning can work wonders and eliminate years of grease and dirt that can accumulate even in the most meticulously clean kitchens. If your cabinets are looking dated or rundown, you do have some alternatives:

- The whole kitchen can look remarkably refreshed by just replacing the doors of the cabinets—not the base on which the doors sit. This is called refacing. Sometimes this process also includes the trim. If you have standard cabinets, this can be a very economical choice.

- Another approach is to paint the cabinets. This requires some work but the difference can be significant for a modest amount of money.

This kitchen is in good shape, but too dark and out-of-date.

(Courtesy of Julie Dana, The Home Stylist)

By painting the cabinets white and the walls a lighter color, the whole kitchen is transformed.

(Courtesy of Julie Dana, The Home Stylist)

◆ Sometimes simply a trendy set of hardware (knobs and pulls) can help update the kitchen's overall appearance.

Floors. Another important kitchen component to examine is the flooring, which can frequently date the kitchen rather quickly. When choosing new floors, stick with medium tones of a neutral color, such as gray or beige, as with the countertops.

Ceramic tile is much more affordable than it once was, particularly if you choose an in-stock pattern at your local home building center. If installing ceramic or porcelain tile, use the biggest size you can find, as it will make the space appear larger. For example, instead of 12 × 12 tiles, consider a 16 × 16 or larger if the room will accommodate. By eliminating the additional tile lines, the room will appear more spacious. For narrow spaces, consider laying the tile on a diagonal which will also give the illusion of size.

Look for something that looks expensive, such as ceramic tile or slate, but is not. Find out what other homeowners are installing these days, and then get the most expensive that fits your budget. Some look like high-end ceramic tiles, but aren't.

If your budget is modest, a sheet of vinyl can make an extreme difference in the perception of the kitchen and the age of the floor. This one change can be well worth the money.

This flooring is dark and dated, definitely in need of being replaced.

(Courtesy of Julie Dana, The Home Stylist)

Easy-to-use peel and stick linoleum tiles brighten the room and bring it into the twenty-first century, for very little money.

(Courtesy of Julie Dana, The Home Stylist)

Appliances. The next issue with kitchens is the appliances. In some parts of the country, it is common for appliances to stay with the home, while in other parts of the country they almost never do. Be aware of these customs in your area and the condition of your appliances—if the buyer will be bringing his or her own, there is less of a need to invest in long-lasting units.

However, if your appliances are avocado green or harvest gold, you should probably get to the store as quickly as possible. If your appliances are more than 20 years old—no matter what the color—you should consider replacing them.

Here are three other economical options:

- ◆ Purchase used models or scratch-and-dent floor models in white or stainless steel. But be sure the dents are on the side that doesn't show.

- ◆ Most appliances can be painted with spray enamel specifically formulated for appliances. Take it outside on a nice day and by dinner you'll have a new appliance.

- ◆ Other appliances can be covered with black or stainless steel-looking sheets that cover the front and sides.

Backsplash and Sink. If you have tiles as your countertop backsplash, check to see if they need regrouting or if they need to be replaced to make them more current.

Sinks should not be leaking anywhere and, most important, should always be sparkling clean.

The kitchen is your money-maker. If you have to choose where to invest a good portion of your remodeling funds for the best possible payout, this is the room in which to do it.

Most kitchen remodeling jobs and many kitchen repairs need to be done by a professional, so check with your town clerk to determine what the requirements are and whether you need a permit before any work begins.

Money Maker _____

If you are replacing kitchen appliances, choose white or stainless appliances for selling your home. If you are in a traditionally warmer area, then white is a good choice. In areas with a true change of seasons, consider off-white, as it can be a stepping stone to a warmer color palette in the room. A warm color scheme will give the feeling of coziness. These colors will generally be the least expensive and you can't ever go wrong with classics.

Bathrooms

Just because bathrooms are typically the smallest rooms in the house doesn't mean they are unimportant. In fact, they are a big factor in the purchase decision. The current trend is creating bathrooms that feel like a retreat or a spa.

Buyers look for bathrooms that are fresh and clean. This means the condition and appearance of the bathtub, toilet, and sink must be spotless.

Toilets. If the toilet is a "decorator" color (also known as retro and themed colors) such as pink, blue, or green, it needs to be removed. Replacing the toilet can usually be done for under $300.

If you cannot replace the toilet, then decorate to the current trends to make it look purposeful. For example, blue is a common older color and by pairing it with tan or brown—a popular color combination currently in fashion—instead of other pastels, such as peach, will make the bathroom look slightly more contemporary.

Bathtubs. Tubs in neutral colors may be just in need of some freshening. Take a good look at the grout in your bathtub area. Is it disgusting? A bleach pen in a well-ventilated room can make a remarkable difference for little money. If the bathtub is also a "decorator" color, you can consider these economical alternatives:

Money Maker

In recent years, large fancy bathtubs were installed to make the bathroom appear higher-end. This trend seems to be declining because people are realizing they just don't have time for a long bath. If you are gutting your bathroom, consider a fancy shower with extra bells and whistles, as it is more practical for most people.

- Tubs can be refaced or resurfaced. A person specialized in this product/service comes to your bathroom and "paints" over the bathtub.

- Bathtubs can also be a covered by a specially-designed sheath. It covers the whole tub and surround. Check your local telephone book for a bathtub refitter near you.

Other aspects of your bathroom, like the flooring, tiles, sink, and vanity, should also be as on-trend as you can make them. Flooring in bathrooms can quickly become ruined with just one or two accidental tub overflows. A new floor may make your bathroom look fresh and modern in one afternoon. Regrouting is also an inexpensive option to help make the bathroom shine. Again, if using ceramic tile or vinyl squares, go for the larger size to give the illusion of size.

Many times calling in a professional plumber or bathroom remodeler is needed because of advanced plumbing needs, tiling, and electricity.

Floors

Flooring tells a lot about how the home is kept. If your carpeting is slightly stained or dirty, a good steam cleaning may be all that is required. You can have the steam cleaning done by professional carpet cleaners or you can rent a steamer from your local store.

If your carpeting is worn and animals have had some house training accidents on it, a better choice is to replace it. No matter what your current carpet color, when you replace it you should choose a real estate beige—it is called that because it complements virtually anyone's furnishings and is preferred by real estate buyers. No one can say "This won't go with my furnishings" while looking at beige flooring.

You can often find a carpeting sale that will allow you to redo several rooms for a reasonable price. If you are replacing carpet in multiple rooms, do NOT change colors. Using the same color throughout will give the home the illusion of space.

Look under the carpet and see if hardwood floors are lurking there. It used to be very common practice to cover hardwood with carpet, but now there is a newfound appreciation for the visual warmth that a wood floor adds. Hardwood floors will also give the potential buyers more decorating options. Hardwood floors that need some TLC are best left for the professionals. Big divots caused by an amateur sanding them will not accentuate the natural beauty of the wood. Finish with a satin coat of urethane to protect the wood and bring out the beauty.

Basements

Not all homes have a basement but if yours does, concentrate on making it clean and dry. These are the two big considerations when it comes to basements. And if you can make it look spacious and show the flexibility of the space, you're in even better shape.

Additions and Add-on Rooms

Home additions are not generally recommended prior to selling, although your real estate agent may be able to advise you regarding whether you could ever hope to recoup your investment. In most cases, you won't, however, unless adding on is the only way to make the home of interest to buyers.

If your home has already had additions made, work to blend the old and new parts of the property as seamlessly as possible. By matching the trim (inside and out), and making the space flow better, it should help, not hurt, your price. Additions are most noticeable when the outside has not been matched to the existing part of the building.

Calling in the Pros

Now that you have a sense of what kinds of remodeling and repair projects may be in your future, let's look at which professionals may be available to help, listed in alphabetical order.

Architect

An architect is the person who is up-to-date on local zoning and building codes and can draw up blueprints for a remodeling contractor to use. Choose an experienced professional who specializes in residential real estate, who has worked on projects like yours.

Bricklayers or Stone Masons

Bricklayers work on laying bricks or stone for walls, floors, and fireplaces.

Carpenters

If wood is involved in your project, you will most likely need a carpenter. They can do a wide range of duties, from framing in walls, building cabinets, to repairing railings. As in any other field, some carpenters are more experienced than others and may even know building codes and engineering (which is a plus!).

Carpet Installers

Carpet installers do not just slap down new carpeting, but often times need to know how to fix the sub floor—the concrete or wood floor underneath the carpeting or hardwoods—so the carpeting lays better. They also need to make the seams connecting separate pieces of carpeting disappear.

Concrete and Cement Workers

These tradespeople work on patios, driveways, and sidewalks primarily. They need to know how to mix cement and how to smooth it for the best appearance. They also know how weather and humidity will affect how the new cement cures—not something a weekend warrior would know.

Contractor

Think of a contractor as the conductor who directs all the individual musicians. They need strong organizational skills in order to manage people and time well. They usually have knowledge in a wide range of home improvement trades to ensure they can hire and supervise all their workers (or subcontractors) for a specific task. A good contractor will save you from buying aspirin in bulk.

Drywall Installers

Drywall is also called sheetrock, gypsum, and wallboard. Drywall installers actually put up walls by fastening them to the wood framing of the structure and join the separate pieces tighter. They also smooth and prep the wall for paint.

Electrician

Most electricians have graduated from an extensive education and training program and passed their state's licensing requirements. These skilled trades people read blueprints, install electrical wiring, and add or repair wires. They can also assess the electricity needs in your home.

Hardwood Floor Specialists

People trained in the area of hardwood floors will sand the floors with large sanding machines and then seal and protect them with specific products. They can make recommendations regarding stains based on the wood type in place. Many sanders will also install hardwood floors.

HVAC Installers

This acronym stands for heating, ventilation, and air conditioning (HVAC) and represents the folks who handle furnace and air conditioning issues. They can also advise you regarding proper ventilation and the capacity of the equipment you need.

Landscape Architect

Landscape architects are the interior designers of your outside space. Their expertise includes soil types and plant sun requirements, to help with new plantings, although they can also draw up plans that will reflect what their recommendations will look like in a few years. Most will subcontract the actual physical labor.

Lawn and Yard Maintenance

These handy people will keep your lawn and yard in top shape with trimming of bushes and mowing of lawns. They are a good idea if you are unable to keep your yard in curb appeal shape.

Painters and Paper Hangers

These skilled people paint the walls and many will also do outside work. They generally prep the walls, such as by scraping off old wallpaper. Paper hangers will hang wallpaper for you, prep walls for painting, and clean up after the painting job.

Plumbers

Plumbers work on and install pipes used for water, waste, and drainage to and from the home. They can install a new sink or toilet as well as help with dishwashers and other water based machines.

Roofers

Yes, they install and repair roofs—everything from shingles to asphalt, slate, and tile. Some roofers also install skylights.

The Least You Need to Know

◆ Do careful research to know how your home compares to your neighbors', and their amenities.

◆ Repair and fix safety issues first.

◆ Make remodeling changes that look high-end but don't have a high price tag.

◆ Many remodeling jobs should be handed over to trained professionals, both to ensure the job is done properly and to keep you safe.

Chapter 7

Curb Appeal

In This Chapter

- ◆ Effects of a charming looking house
- ◆ How the driveway and roof impact curb appeal
- ◆ Little details add up to big impact
- ◆ Making your house desirable

Curb appeal is not a new concept. We know you have heard about it, but you may be asking yourself, what exactly do I have to do to achieve curb appeal? In this chapter, we will give you tricks and tips to make your home so desirable on the outside, that potential buyers just can't wait to see what's inside. We want to make them crave your home!

What Exactly Is Curb Appeal?

When searching for a place, more than 72 percent of people visit desirable neighborhoods either physically or virtually in search of their dream home. They may also look at MLS listings and photos in greater detail to determine if it's really worth their time to check out the inside of a property if the outside doesn't really draw them in.

You may have thought curb appeal was about putting a nice pot of flowers on the front stoop, but in fact, it is much more than that. Curb appeal is all about the overall impression of the front of your home, which includes the driveway, roof, the building's exterior, and your front lawn—everything someone sees as they look at it from the curb. Curb appeal is also about the doghouse and the spotted, patchy lawn next to it (which is less appealing).

There is one very important fact to know and to keep repeating in your head: prospective buyers will formulate an opinion about your home in the first 15 seconds. No, that is not a typo—it is 15 seconds, not 15 minutes. If you don't "wow" them immediately, you will have a harder time selling your home.

The key with curb appeal is that the 15 seconds begin as soon as your home comes into view for people driving by. Not only are they looking quickly, since their eyes are also paying attention to the road, but they see one side first, then the front, and then the other side, all in a matter of seconds. Scouting potential homes can also occur when people are taking a nice leisurely walk through the area. The 15-second rule still applies, though they'll have a little more time to confirm their impression. Just imagine the conversation.

In the best possible scenario, you'd hear:

"Isn't that house adorable? Look, even the front door is spectacular. Let's call our agent right now."

Money Maker

Sometimes there is nothing you can do about a crumbling sidewalk in front of your house, especially if it's maintained by your city, but you can make sure it is neat and clean. Pull up any weeds, sweep it off, and edge the grass on either side to make it look as well maintained as possible.

Or, when the home isn't so appealing, even from the curb:

"That house is okay. Did you see that front garden? It sure needs watering. By the way, did you pay our water bill?"

Curb appeal sets expectations. Just by looking at your home, people will decide if it is a fixer upper, or a meticulously clean property worth every penny you're asking for. Granted, that impression may be off, but a buyer's initial assessment will determine if they are willing to continue to consider purchasing it.

The great thing about curb appeal is that it doesn't necessarily cost a lot of money if you're willing to do most of the work yourself. Usually one solid Saturday can get a typical home in curb appeal form. Of course, some homes will require a little more work, but we'll walk you through that in a moment.

By investing time to boost your home's curb appeal, it has a better chance of selling faster and for your asking price.

Driveways

Most of us don't give much thought to our driveway, but if you have one, you'll want to spiff it up. A driveway can be a gleaming advantage or a major eyesore, depending on what you do (or don't) to it.

Depending on your driveway type, a good cleaning to remove oil stains can work wonders. If your driveway is asphalt, a fresh coating of sealant will make it look like new. A gravel driveway may just need a new load of rocks to freshen its appearance. If your cement driveway is in really bad shape—more than 50 percent of it has potholes or is crumbling—it's probably worth the money to have it replaced. Bottom line is to clean and recoat, replenish if appropriate, or replace if it's in really bad shape.

For greater curb appeal, the next step with the driveway is to edge it, by making a crisp, clean cut between the lawn and the edge of the driveway. This extra step creates a clean and tidy impression.

While you have the edger out, trim the sidewalk and path to the doors or garage, too, if you have any. Although you may not normally keep your lawn and driveway so meticulous, this extra step while the house is on the market will help dramatically.

When you picture a very long driveway, what comes to mind? Higher-end houses and fancy estates, right? People equate long driveways with upscale properties. No matter how long your driveway is, you can make it seem longer by keeping your car in the garage. With no cars in the driveway, it elongates the appearance.

In your driveway, are there basketball hoops or big wheel tricycles? Of course, children need to play, but just be sure that toys are put away when they are finished. If the basketball net is beyond repair, replace it, or take it down. You never know when someone will drive by to take a look and you don't want hockey nets and skateboard ramps in the driveway to distract them.

Staging Snafu

"I have known people to drive around the block to get a look at the back yard of a house, but when there is a bunch of useless bikes and construction material stashed behind the garage, it ruins the sale."
—Stephanie Morgan, licensed real estate sales agent

Sidewalks

Sidewalks can also either add or detract from your curb appeal. What you'll want to do next is take a look at the path most prospective buyers will take to your door.

Most of the time, a real estate agent and potential buyer will drive to your home and park the car in the driveway or on the street. What happens next? They walk to the front door.

However, you and your family probably use the side or back door more frequently, and you may not realize that the pathway or sidewalk is no longer in presentable shape. Now is your chance to clean it up.

Another common problem with the pathway to the front door is that shrubs have overgrown it and you can no longer easily walk on it without getting brushed by branches. It's time to pull out the hedge trimmers to cut back any bushes or plantings that are obscuring the view of the sidewalk, or are impeding the path.

Sidewalks and driveways also need to be kept cleaned and clear, no matter what the season. During winter in northern states, be sure to keep your sidewalk shoveled at all times—it makes it so welcoming and easy to walk on. Make that first impression count!

The same holds true for fall leaves—even though you may personally love crunching through the colorful leaves, buyers may not. Make your sidewalk as welcoming to buyers as possible.

With a plain house and tired shrubs, this house has little to offer.

(Courtesy of Nanette Catarinella, Room Styles Interiors)

The house gets a new front door color, new shrubs, and cleaned walkway for an improved appeal.

(Courtesy of Nanette Catarinella, Room Styles Interiors)

If you do not have a walkway to your front door, you do not have to add an expensive concrete sidewalk. Your local home improvement store has beautiful large pavers, landscaping tiles, or bricks that will work for your path. You will first need to level the ground and dig it out slightly for the tiles to lay in the ground flat, but it is certainly cheaper than other options.

For the very best impression and curb appeal, have an inviting and clear path to your front door. Just a little elbow grease with your hedge clippers and edger can make your home more appealing in less than a couple hours.

House Color

If the paint on the exterior of your home is flaking or faded, or the siding has seen better days, now is the perfect time to put on a fresh coat of paint or take care of replacing the worn siding. It will be well worth the investment.

The trick is choosing a color that will be admired by the largest percentage of home buyers—you wouldn't want to invest in a new coat of paint only to hear buyers exclaiming, "Too bad we'll need to have it painted as soon as we move in," which is much more likely if you go with a wild color, like bright purple or dark teal, for example.

The safest bet for paint or siding is a neutral color, such as white, beige, light gray, or cream.

This means if your home is currently a dark or unusual color, it may be in your best interest to change it. "Ouch," you say, but the reality is that if you want to sell your house fast and for the most money, it cannot be a unique color.

There was a house in a nearby town we call "the very blue house." Did you notice that we called it "the very blue house," not just blue? That's because it was that electric, bright blue. And when it went up for sale, it took a very long time to sell. Of course, as soon as the new owners moved in, they painted it. That particular home took a while to sell because it is hard to find special people who can look beyond the electric blue, and know they will have a big job when they take possession of the house.

If you have vinyl siding, a good power washing might be all that is needed to make your home sparkle again. If you have a brick exterior, you are most likely getting off easy. If you have a stucco house, it can be tricky to match and blend old stucco with the new, so rely on professionals for this kind of work.

Trim and Accent Color

So back to your house. Choosing a color for the body of the house is simple—neutral colors—but the trim, shutters and doors can be a little trickier.

Here is the rule to follow: the more symmetrical your home, the sharper contrast you can go with for trim and accent colors. For example, if your house is a front entrance colonial with center door and two windows on each side of the door, you can have a sharp contrast like a white body with black shutters. If your home is more asymmetrical, where windows are not lined up with each other well, you should have less contrast between the body and trim paint colors. For instance, a raised ranch with dormers and a side addition looks better with low contrast such as a medium cream body and light tan trim.

Money Maker

If you still can't figure out what color to paint the trim, there are a few websites that can help. For example, Benjamin Moore paint company has the "personal color viewer" system in which you can import a photo of a room or the entire exterior of your home, and then apply different paint shades to see which you like the most. Learn more at: www.benjaminmoore.com.

Many times the body of your home doesn't need be repainted, but a fresh coat of trim paint can make your home sparkle like new. Our next door neighbor had a soft butter yellow house with brown trim—boy, did it scream 1970s. But by painting the brown trim white, the home was quickly brought up-to-date.

One of the best ways to find a paint color that is stylish is to turn to the experts—real estate developers. Look for model homes in new housing developments in your area. Homes built in the last few years by developers, not individuals, are "in the know" for the most current color combinations that people want to purchase. They have done the research in your particular area and your part of the country. Go ahead and copy their colors. They sell those nice big houses for big money and you want to, too. One trick is to use three colors on your home, which gives it the look of a more expensive home: simply paint the front door in an accent color to the trim and siding.

The Roof

Unless it leaks, your roof is probably something that you don't really think about too much. But your roof can still have a big impact on curb appeal. When preparing your home for sale, be sure to take a look up there. Are there Frisbees resting on the roof? Did some small branches or pinecones fall on it? Is moss growing on some parts? In addition to cleaning off the roof, be sure to clean out the gutters, too.

If you doubt that a roof can play a part in the total curb appeal of your house, look at the house across the street from you. If their roof was, oh, let's say orange, how much of the visual snapshot of the home would be orange? The roof probably accounts for a good one-third or one-half of the total image—not a pretty picture, is it? Think of the power of the old Howard Johnson's signature orange roof or McDonald's red roof. The big corporations realize that roofs get noticed.

If you find you have to replace the roof before selling your home, you'll want to pay close attention to the color of your home when choosing the color of your new roof—some exterior paint and roof colors just don't go well together. It is best to play it safe and go with a gray, brown, or black roof. You really can't go wrong with classic colors.

A family recently hired me to help prepare their home for sale. As I was doing a house review, I quickly noticed that there were two roof shingles that needed to be replaced. How did that happen I asked? The couple told me that their family cat would climb up on the roof and scratch at the window to be let in. While it was up there, it would use the shingles as a scratching post. Those two shingles really stood out and a simple replacement job was all that was needed to get the whole roof looking new again.

Doors

Doors also play a huge part in the curb appeal of a home. A door can be dramatic, with lead glass and insets, or it can be solid, painted in a magnificent color. When staging your home to sell, focus on getting your door in ship shape for inspection.

Staging Snafu _____

Don't ignore your front entryway. Studies have shown that the one place buyers stand the longest is at the front entrance, waiting for their agent to open the door. Potential buyers have a chance to glance around and form an opinion even before the door is open and they step a foot into the house. Don't pass up this opportunity to really impress them by making sure everything near the front door is perfect.

Regarding doors, the first thing you should consider is which door potential buyers will enter first. Almost always it is the front door, despite the fact that it is not the door the family regularly uses.

In a number of cases, I have been called in to stage a home after it has been on the market a while without any interest. One of the first things I do is check which door people are entering. In one case, the real estate agent picked the door closest to the driveway, which makes logical sense, but doesn't give the greatest first impression. When you open that door you first see the steps going to the basement—not all that attractive—and you also see the back of the kitchen where they keep trash and recyclables, another less than impressive view. But when we switched the location of the lockbox to the front door, agents and buyers were greeted by a formal foyer with a grand piano in the side room. Much better!

However, the opposite can also work, depending on the view out the back. Sometimes taking the buyer to the back door, where they catch a glimpse of the breath-taking panoramic view, can seal the deal before you even cross the threshold.

There are a couple of things you can easily do to give your door maximum curb appeal.

The first thing is to see if the doors need painting. (Remember buyers are waiting there.) Don't forget to paint all your doors, including the side and back doors. You might only seldom use them, but they can get dirty and stained just by being exposed to the outdoors. Choose a color that complements your existing color scheme.

The second thing to do is to be sure your trees and bushes are well trimmed, so potential buyers get a completely unobstructed view of the front door. This provides the most appealing and welcoming entrance for your home. I know you may think, "But those bushes have been there for 20 years…." Yes, but they looked great 15 years ago and now they are just too big. Ask yourself if you want the bushes to dominate the view of your home, or if you'd rather people notice the front door. You don't necessarily have to rip the bushes out, but trimming them way back would serve you well.

Thirdly, make sure that the screen or storm door matches the shape of the front door. For example, if your screen door has the glass down one third of the way, but your main door has glass half way down, the mismatch makes the door look like it has crooked teeth.

Before: There may be a home behind this shrubbery, but potential buyers can't see it.

(Courtesy of StagedHomes.com)

After: Cutting the bushes and trees back reveals a beautiful front yard and eye-catching doorway with plenty of curb appeal.

(Courtesy of StagedHomes.com)

While we are talking about doors, it's a good idea to check out your doorbell. Do you know if it still works? Make sure that it does. Buyers have been known to test it to see if it works and if it doesn't, it makes a bad first impression.

Replacement doorbells are easy to find and now easy to install. (In fact my 7-year-old son put ours in.) Shine up that doorknocker, too. A small gesture like that can make your door sparkle to perspective shoppers. While you are standing there, look down. How is the threshold? Is it beat up? Does it have ground-in dirt? Investing a little time to spiff it up will be well worth it.

All Hands On Deck

Decks and porches also need to be repaired and presentable. Depending on your location, outdoor decks and porches are a large part of community and family life. You generally do not have to add or totally remodel a porch or deck if you are selling, but your existing one does have to look attractive and safe. This does not have to be a big job but a good scrub-down can help a lot. Sometimes simply a light sanding and reapplying sealer or stain will do all that is needed to freshen it up.

Your local home improvement store can show you what specific products are best to use on your type of deck or porch. You can also contact a carpenter to fix any broken railings or steps. Your porch or deck can set you apart from other houses, but only if it is in nice shape. Make sure you accentuate this unique selling point.

Money Maker

Every year *Remodeling* magazine produces a comprehensive cost-versus-value report. It compares construction costs with the value the work adds to the resale of the house. This report breaks the data down by city and region. It also compares up-scale remodels versus mid-range priced projects. Take a look at this year's issue at www. remodeling.hw.net before undertaking any major additions.

Pools and Water Features

If you don't have a pool or fountain, don't put one in. If you have an older above-ground pool, it is probably best to completely take it out and plant sod or quick growing grass seed. If you have an in-ground pool, it needs to be in working order with clear, fresh water—blackish greenish water will not help your sale.

The only exception—and this is where your homework will pay off—is if just about all the homes in your neighborhood have a pool. In some areas of the country, and even within certain housing developments, an in-ground pool is almost a standard feature. You will probably not get your money out of it but, in those areas, having one will make your house sell sooner.

Ponds and water fountains are also very popular now. If the fountain is not imbedded and is portable, it will be considered personal property and you can plan to take the fountain with you. A small man-made pond can often turn off a buyer, just as a pool does because of upkeep and liability. It will probably be worth the expense to take the pond out and fill it in to draw a wider range of potential buyers.

In general, adding a water feature will not improve your odds of selling your home faster or for more money.

Accessorize to Impress

Now that you've tackled all the must-do's, it's time to jazz up your place. Home accessories are those nice details that give a house that pulled-together, ready-for-an-open-house look.

What's Your Number?

Start by taking a look at your home from the road. Can you see your house number? Do you have to know where to look to find it? If so, that's not good. And is the number in a contrasting color? Brass numbers on a cream house are hard to see, as are any numbers spelled out in cursive.

You want your house number to be large and easy-to-find, which makes it easier to sell your home. How, you ask? If a potential buyer sees your place and likes the curb appeal enough to want to see the inside, they will call their real estate agent to make arrangements to see it. The call from the prospective buyer would go something like this if the number is unclear:

Buyer: "I would like to see the darling beige Cape-style house that is on Main Street."

Agent: "Sure, is that the house at 123 Main? Or the one at 987 Main Street? It's funny, but that description also fits a house at 8001 Main Parkway. Are you sure you're on Main?"

Or, when the number is clear:

Buyer: "I would like to see the house at 123 Main Street.

Agent: "Sure, let's make an appointment."

A bonus of having a prominent, easy-to-find property number is that flower and pizza deliveries will arrive fresh. And more important, emergency vehicles won't drive by it.

Mailboxes

Have you picked up your mail today? Have you taken a close look at your mailbox? How old is it? Is it rusted? Maybe it has peeling paint? Your mailbox is an extension of your home, so make sure it's just as up-to-date and spotless.

Welcome Mat

One quick, easy, and inexpensive update is a new welcome mat for your front landing. Get rid of your ratty old one and put down a bright, fresh one to greet any buyers.

Adornments

The most common mistake people make at their front entrance area is too much "stuff." Wreaths, for instance, can be very tricky. Even though they are very pretty most of the time, they should be removed for staging because they can quickly date a house and emphasize the wrong style. This includes a Christmas wreath in January or an out-of-date wreath that has an extra large draping bow.

In addition to the overgrown bush blocking the view of the front door, this home's list of "don'ts" includes a string of holiday lights still up on the porch, and a mismatched screen and interior door.

(Courtesy of Julie Dana, The Home Stylist)

If your wreath is more than two years old, it's time to move it on. Wreaths change style just like flower arrangement trends. The good news is, you can use it in your next home if you really can't bear to part with it.

Occasional flags are another touchy subject, and we end up on the side of no decorative banners, such as a scene of a sandcastle in the summer, or a little drummer boy in December. This is a personal style statement that you don't want to impose on others.

Flower baskets, containers, and pots on the porches usually look very nice, but only if they are bright and bushy with colorful flowers. Depending on your climate, it can take one day for your flowers to go from perky to droopy.

Make the first impression bright, cheery, and well-kept, so buyers will be confident that the entire home is well taken care of.

And you'll definitely want to remove birdfeeders, wind chimes, weather vanes, and lawn ornaments, no matter how beautiful. For some buyers, they look like clutter, and can prevent them from seeing anything else, just like indoor clutter. And we don't want anything to distract a buyer from seeing the house. This doesn't mean you shouldn't put them right back up in your new place, but to stage a home, you need to pack them up and put them away.

Lighting

Thankfully, lighting is usually easy to do and can make your house inviting at the flick of a switch. Here are a few tips:

Make sure your bulbs are not burned out in your front porch light, near all your outside doors, or your garage area.

An easy, but dramatic, lighting addition is the installation of small solar lights placed along the pathway to your doorway.

Money Maker

Speaking of porch lights, another easy way to reflect more light is to paint the inside ceiling of your porch. This helps in two ways. It reflects your entry light to make it brighter than it really is. Painting the ceiling also makes light reflect into the house for a brighter look inside, too.

Remember that people could drive by at any time of day or night. Is your house visible at night? What does the curb appeal show after it gets dark? Although it is not the most energy efficient advice, we recommend keeping your outside lights on most of the time when the house is on the market. It makes for a welcoming look—just as you would put the porch light on if a guest is expected.

Pets

The difficult truth is that a home with pets can sometimes be the hardest to stage. But don't worry, there a couple simple things you can do to get even nonanimal lovers to like your place.

The first thing to look at, if you have a dog, is the condition of your lawn. Most dogs relieve themselves on their own lawn, which creates yellow patches here and there. The staging secret—now don't laugh at this—is spray paint. Yes, get a can of green spray paint, matching your grass color as close as possible, and spray away the patchy area.

You'll also want to be on constant alert when your dog leaves droppings, so you can immediately pick up and dispose of them properly. Picking it up regularly cuts down on odor, flies, and the possibility of dirty shoes. Buyers will walk in the yard to get a better view of the outside, so make sure there can be no missteps.

If you store your pet's food and water bowls outdoors, you'll also want to pick those up and store them temporarily, too.

Your beloved pet's outdoor house may need some attention, too. Does it need washing or painting? Many buyers, especially animal lovers, will take the condition of your animal area as a sign of how meticulous you are about everything you own—which is good.

And if you have a doggy door or cat door in any of your house doors, you'll want to make sure it's sparkling clean, too.

If you are selling a farm with animal stalls and pens, be sure to keep the barn and stalls clean and fresh, too. Make an impression with a super clean barn and you'll win them over nearly every time.

Landscaping

The condition, health, and style of your plantings and foliage can either encourage people to look at your home or discourage them from it. Let's look at how landscaping helps shape the impression buyers have of your home.

In today's society, where so many houses are cookie-cutter designs, styled all the same in a neighborhood, you can set yours apart with awesome landscaping. The old days of two bushes on each side of the door are gone. In their place is landscaping, with a slightly less formal feel and an increasingly asymmetrical look. Today's trends are for a slightly winding front path, rather than a direct straight shot to the door. This more casual, relaxed feel doesn't mean scattered and untidy, however.

This small cottage needs attention to detail to make it appealing.

(Courtesy of Linda Pellien, Home Finishing Touches)

With a new exterior and bright flowers, the house is ready for new owners.

(Courtesy of Linda Pellien, Home Finishing Touches)

Of course, you know you should weed. This includes your front garden, if you have one, and your lawn. The easiest thing to do after you weed is to make sure weeds don't grow back by covering the area with mulch, ground foliage, or even gravel in some geographic areas. There are plenty of weed-killing products on the market, too, including organic and environmentally friendly varieties to choose from.

Mulch is one of my favorite curb appeal tricks—spreading a bag of mulch changes a distinctive area of land from dull to dynamite in a matter of a half an hour. It gives a finished appearance to the area. First you may want to try simply raking the mulch you had applied last year, however, because mixing the mulch up can make it appear you had a whole new application, without the bill.

Dead Trees/Piles of Junk. Remove dead trees that are on your property. Large trees should be removed by a professional, not only because they are unpredictable and dangerous, but because buyers will be hesitant to purchase your home knowing they will already have a to-do list. It also makes people wonder what else you're not dealing with, if you couldn't even have an obviously dead tree removed.

You'll also want to remove any piles of junk from behind the garage. You might need to rent a dumpster but it will be well worth the cost in terms of additional potential buyers.

Add Color. If you are purchasing a cluster of flowering plants as decoration, get them as colorful and long lasting as you can. Ask your local nursery what lasts the longest. Buyers love to see fresh colorful blooms—it makes them happy, and happy people buy homes. Add two simple pots of flowers on each side of the front door, or on the steps leading to the front entrance. Make people smile. You can never go wrong with geraniums, mums, marigolds, and impatiens, which are all available in a variety of colors. Also, keep in mind that your flower pots should mirror your home's style. If your home is more formal, then the flowers in your pots should reflect that. A cottage style home should have more casual flowers.

While you are digging near your house, take a glance around. Do you think a piece of latticework covering the crawl space beneath the porch would help dress it up? It probably would.

Also, what color is your foundation? If your house color can tolerate it, paint the foundation green because as the bushes are filling in, the green background will make them appear more lush and full.

Play Equipment. Are your children grown but their sandbox is still in the back yard? Has the large plastic dollhouse seen better days? All the dated and rusty playground equipment should be removed from your yard.

If your target market would be a family with small children, creating a play area is a positive unless it makes the backyard seem smaller.

If your plastic play items are still in use, but don't look the greatest, don't despair.

They now make specifically formulated spray paint for plastic. With just a little effort, your child's favorite climbing gym will look brand new, and will be perfect to show off in your immaculate back yard.

Mowing the Lawn. Mowing your lawn on a regular basis to keep it trimmed and tidy is pretty much a given, but did you know that the best direction in which to mow your lawn is on the diagonal? By cutting the grass in a diagonal pattern, you make it appear longer and wider.

Sale Sign. The most important thing you should know about a "For Sale" sign is that when you place it in the yard can be a point of negotiation with a real estate agent. Sure, sign the Realtor contract, but don't officially open it for showings until every bit of your home is staged and ready for inspection.

If you put the sign out too soon, before you've finished all your work, then eager buyers won't get the best first impression. Part of selling your home is creating the "buzz" and "word-of-mouth" about how great your home is. You don't want the word to get out that your home is not all that great, needs updating, has no storage space, and rooms need painting. Get it ready and then put the sign out.

The Least You Need to Know

- ◆ Make sure the driveway, sidewalk, and pathways are inviting and cleared.

- ◆ Choose a neutral color for the main exterior of your house. Copy trim colors from newly built homes in the area.

- ◆ Trim away excess foliage and keep exterior accessories to a minimum to show off the house.

- ◆ Make your front door the star it should be, to impress buyers.

Part 3

Room by Room

Now that we have the basics taken care of, we will attack each room individually, figuring out what needs to be done to get buyers to fall in love with your home.

In addition to pointing out trouble spots to be aware of, we'll give you specific staging secrets for each room or space to make it irresistible to buyers. We will also help you figure out what to do if you don't have a particular type of room.

Most important, we'll make staging each room fun and easy, with inexpensive tricks of the trade worth thousands.

8

The Entrances and Exits

In This Chapter

- ◆ Making the foyer the best it can be
- ◆ "Wow" them with the view
- ◆ Addressing stairs and hallways
- ◆ The backdoor—leave a lasting impression

The purpose of a foyer, or entryway, is to introduce your home. When you are staging your home, the foyer is the first impression buyers get of the interior. The backdoor area is the last impression they remember. Staging these two areas can properly accent the home's appeal and make people want to buy it.

The First Interior Impression

Because the foyer can be such a busy place, you may not have noticed that it doesn't have the most current look. By making it special, not only can you make visitors feel immediately at ease, but you can start potential buyers off on the right foot.

What They See

You want buyers' first impression of your home to be of a stylish, up-to-date, welcoming place. You want them to see it as organized and clean—somewhere they'd be comfortable living. The foyer sets the tone for the whole home. What kind of first impression is your home giving? Maybe the hall closet has not had a working door in a while, or maybe it is so stuffed with coats it won't close. This gives an immediate impression that there is not enough storage space.

Maybe your foyer has wallpaper or stenciling on it that you love but may be dated or not as appealing to others as it is to you. Everyone's taste is different and someone coming into your home for the first time may presume that your whole home is styled in this manner. Do you want a potential buyer's first impression to be of all the work they'll need to do to make it their own? Probably not.

Getting Through the Eye of the Needle

When buyers view a home, they are usually accompanied by a real estate agent. Most often buyers come in pairs and are sometimes accompanied by children or a trusted friend. On any given viewing, you can have two people or six people entering your home at the same time. How easy is that to do in your foyer? Many entryways can get a little cramped.

This large table topped with several family photos makes the room seem smaller and too personal.

(Courtesy of Mary McDonald, Re-Creating Interiors)

Take a look at your foyer and entryway with an eye for making it easier for people to enter your home. Maybe you need to replace the large foyer table with a skinnier one, or maybe remove the table altogether for more space.

Replacing the table with a more impressive table featuring an inviting display makes the foyer more comfortable.

(Courtesy of Mary McDonald, Re-Creating Interiors)

Make sure the traffic flow is adequate for the groups coming into your entryway. If a table or other piece of furniture is blocking progress into the other parts of your home, repositioning it or replacing it could make the traffic flow work better.

Updating and styling this relatively small room can make a better first impression for potential buyers.

Spend Money Here

If you have a limited budget and can only afford to replace the entryway flooring or the guest bedroom carpeting—choose the foyer. It is the first impression. With any luck and proper staging, the buyers will immediately fall in love with your home and by the time they get up to the last room—they want the home, no matter what.

Wow them now! Usually foyers and entryways are of minimal size, so painting it or updating it can be easy and affordable, but will give you a good return on that money.

Make Minor Repairs

The very first thing buyers will see as they enter your home is the flooring. What type of shape is it in? If it's less than five years old it's probably in decent shape. And if it's not, it is definitely worth updating or upgrading the flooring here.

And how about the rug, if you have one. This should not be the standard rough "wipe your feet off" welcome mat, but a real rug. If you don't have one, or the one you do have is in poor shape, check out some of your options at your local home improvement store, or at a carpet outlet.

The next area to review for potential repairs is the lighting. Can you quickly and easily turn on a light in the foyer? Remember that there could be times when your home is shown after dark.

That foyer light, usually an overhead, is a bright and welcoming feature. Are the shades of the light clean? Do you need to dust or clean the chandelier? Does it need to be a more up-to-date look?

Declutter and Clean

Just like any other room in your home, you want your foyer sparkling clean. And some areas of your foyer get dirtier quicker than others. One of those areas that gets filthy usually without anyone even noticing is the threshold—the area you step over to come into the home. To make it sparkle, scrub hard within the grooves to make a great first impression.

While you have the cleaning products out, shine up that doorknob in and out. And the light switch plate by the door. You don't want grape jelly as their first impression.

If yours is like most households, the foyer gets easily cluttered. It is natural for mail and keys and shoes to congregate in this little area. When you declutter it, be sure to remove your personal mail, throw out junk mail, and stash the keys in a subtle location, like a nearby drawer. Some people have a "no shoes on inside the home" rule. That is okay, but there should not be a pile of shoes sitting by the front door. One or two nicely aligned pairs are okay, but it would be even better if you'd put them in a nearby closet.

Coats are another source of clutter. If you have kids and they are like ours, constant nagging is required to remind them to hang up their coats in the closet.

Shoes in the entrance hall is the first thing you see.

(Courtesy of Amy Ross and Beth Sammarone, The Redesign Team)

Tasteful accents and simple changes make the entrance charming.

(Courtesy of Amy Ross and Beth Sammarone, The Redesign Team)

Staging Snafu _____

You may want to think twice about requesting that people who are touring your home take off their shoes. It makes some people uncomfortable and aggravated. You may think that people will think, "Oh, this home must be so clean," but it makes more people irritated than it does impressed. If you have a pair of shoes at the door, some people may get the message, but some won't.

Foyer Arrangement and Style Choices

As you stage your home, each room will have a clear decorating message that you are trying to achieve. The foyer needs to have a certain look that signals to buyers that this home is worth every penny. What's the look? Visualize a fancy hotel lobby and see if your foyer gives you the same welcoming feeling.

Hotel lobbies are basically large foyers, and are an instant indicator of what kind of room you should expect upstairs. When you are spending a lot of money per night, you want that fancy look as soon as you walk in the doors. The same thing is true of a home. Someone will spend a lot of money for your home, you hope, so make them feel they are getting a good value for their money.

Back to that fancy hotel lobby. What do you see? Usually it is simple elegance—a room that is tastefully decorated but nothing too personal or blatantly promotional. Okay, Donald Trump may be an exception here, but most upscale hotels don't beat you over the head with their corporate name. Likewise, in your own home, you don't want to beat buyers over the head with pictures of your family. Nor do buyers want to see stacks of your mail or piles of stinky shoes—items that are way too personal. A spacious look and welcoming feeling is what you are after.

Keep the décor neutral though. You do not want your style message to be strong in a certain motif, such as roosters or pink or a bold abstract painting. If your buyers have an aversion to country or modern or pink, you just tuned them off and they have only taken one step in the door.

Fortunately, there are some style impressions you can add that will make the foyer special and memorable:

- **Thin table.** An entry table or sofa table can set the tone for the décor. It immediately adds a focal point and useful function to this space.

- **Lamp.** A small lamp on this entry table gives a welcoming signal. The lamp provides a warmer, more inviting light than just an overhead light. Speaking of lighting, be sure to take a hard look at the ceiling or wall light fixtures. Are they dated, pitted, tarnished? It may be time to replace them.

◆ **Seating.** If your entry area can handle a bench or chair without getting crowded, use one. It sends a message that the foyer is large enough to allow guests to sit down to remove shoes.

◆ **Storage.** If your entryway has the space, showing storage immediately is a bonus. This could be an armoire or even pretty baskets under the lower shelf of the entry table.

◆ **Organization.** If the first impression you give is of organization, you can win them. Use pretty trays for mail (don't let it pile up). A sleek bowl for keys shows function.

◆ **Color.** Of course, the colors of the walls should be neutral, but adding a splash of color via a vase of flowers is a winner. Fresh flowers are always better than silk or dried flowers.

> **Experts Explain**
>
> A decorator's trick is to transfer color from the outside to inside. For example, if you have large pots of bright red begonias beside your front door, then on the entry hall table, place a bouquet of bright red flowers. It helps to visually connect the outside to the inside.

If You Don't Have a Foyer ...

Depending on the style layout of your home, you may not have a formal entrance way or foyer. Sometimes the front door opens right into the living room or other room. Don't despair. There are a couple of easy solutions to this.

To create an entryway, simply arrange the furniture so that beside the door is a functioning table and light. Although this may just be your end table, you can accessorize it like you would an entry table. It could also be a sofa table behind your sofa. Treat it and dress it up like a formal entrance way the best you can.

If you have a back or side entrance, you will want it to show function and beauty, too, so dress those areas for sale as well.

If your entryway is small and the only accessories that will fit are a rug and maybe a picture, then by all means, make them really count. Splurge on a smart looking rug. However, if one of the main selling features of the space is the beautiful hardwood floor, do not cover one inch of it with a rug. Hang your most beautiful art on the wall. Make sure that entry light is up to date. Then open the door to buyers.

Room with a View

We are going to let you in on a little professional staging secret: the secret to "wow-ing" buyers is the view. Not the view to the outside, but the all-encompassing first view the buyers have of your home when they walk in the door.

To help you see exactly what the buyer sees, take out a camera and take some pictures. Stand in the doorway and take several shots of the view you see. You will probably need to take them from several angles and take a couple steps inside, too.

You may assume you know what you'll see in those pictures, but don't pre-judge the view. Really take a look at the pictures you've taken. Here are some things to notice and fix before buyers appear on your doorstep:

◆ Do you see the backside of any media appliance, such as a large TV or stereo? Adjust the placement so you don't.

◆ Do you see the back of a couch or loveseat? This can make a buyer feel you are blocking them out.

◆ Can you get a clean shot of the room's focal point, such as the fireplace or the picture window? Can the room's furniture configuration be adjusted so you can?

◆ Are there any doors that are better left open or closed to improve the view, such as a French door leading to a living room?

◆ Is there distracting clutter on top of bookcases, refrigerators, or armoires that you forgot about? You'll want to clear that off.

◆ Can accessories be tweaked to make a better appearance? Simply moving the couch pillows can make all the difference, or add a soft throw to the back of a chair.

Staging Snafu

Real estate agents, if you are reading this, be sure to get out of the way of your buyers. Are you selling your backside, or the home? Often, agents unintentionally block the selling view.

Now that you have seen the pictures, change what you can to make the view better and then take some more. You now have your own set of "before" and "after" room makeover photos!

Stairways and Hallways to Get You Places

If you are like most people, you really don't give much thought to your stairways and hallways. They simply get you where you need to go. Every area is an opportunity to either impress or disappoint a potential buyer. Remember that a disappointed buyer is one who is dropping the potential bid they may give you for your place. By altering even these overlooked spaces, buyers will be impressed.

Make It Functional and Clutter-Free

In both hallways and up stairways, there is plenty of wall space to hang pictures. Art is fine, but be sure you do not have a large grouping of family photos to distract the buyers. Less is always more when staging, so consider one or two large pieces of art instead of a grouping.

A collection of family photos on the stair landing is distracting to buyers.

(Courtesy of Amy Ross and Beth Sammarone, The Redesign Team)

Replacing personal photos with a single piece of art creates a focal point.

(Courtesy of Amy Ross and Beth Sammarone, The Redesign Team)

Although placing things on the stairs until the next person goes upstairs is a common strategy for getting them back to their rightful place, you'll want to clear your stairs of anything in transit. Not only do you want the space clutter-free, but you don't want a buyer tripping in your home.

> **Experts Explain**
>
> "Even when used in small doses, foliage and flowers can lift a room from lifeless to lively."
> —From Christi Carter's *Art of Accessorizing*

Make sure the banister up your stairs is sturdy, clean, and attractive. If you have carpeting or carpet runners on your steps, make sure they are secure. In hallways it is usually best not to have any rugs— you want a clean look. Scatter or throw rugs tend to create visual clutter and make the area seem smaller. And always remember what each space is selling. If you have beautiful floors, don't cover them. Hallways and stairways tend to be dim, so be sure your lights work, and use the strongest wattage possible.

Stylish Additions

Adding style to these areas is easy and fairly inexpensive:

◆ A mirror at the end of the hallway helps add brightness and depth.

◆ Painting the hall trim and wall color nearly the same color helps calm and unify the space.

The lack of any furniture or wall hangings in this space leaves buyers feeling cold. Not a great first impression.

(Courtesy of Amy Ross and Beth Sammarone, The Redesign Team)

The addition of a soft rug, thin bench, small table, and artwork add personality and style to this small space.

(Courtesy of Amy Ross and Beth Sammarone, The Redesign Team)

- A handsome clock is always a good alternative to artwork.

- Consider removing some furniture in the hallway, such as bookcases or tables, to make it feel more spacious.

- Doorways to bedrooms off the hallway should not have nameplates.

- Light switch plates on stairs and hallways should be plain. Save the decorative switch plates for your next home.

Exit, Staging, Right!

As you know, one of the last areas a potential buyer will see is the back door, mudroom, or back vestibule area. This will be the last visual image they will carry with them as they view other homes and compare yours to the competition. Don't neglect this opportunity to impress.

Usually the back or side door is the "family and friends" door. It does tend to have a more casual feel and that's okay. You want your home to be a showplace, but also show it can function well for the buyers.

Staging Snafu

I know someone who did not buy a home because they read the calendar near the back door showing a painter scheduled to paint over water stains and fire damage. Be careful of what your calendar says about you and your home. Buyers can be very nosey.

Generally all this area needs is to be clean and clutter-free. Here are a couple tips to get you going:

- **Command center.** As any busy person will attest, keeping a calendar, message center, and to-do list visible helps the household function smoothly. Yes, you can have these out, but keep the clutter to a minimum.

- **Recyclable/returnable area.** Yes, this area can be a pain to keep under control. Assign someone in your home to be in charge of getting these items out of the home regularly.

- **Shoes and coats.** Some coats or jackets will be in your closet, but if you have hooks, be sure just to keep one or two items there. More than that looks cluttered, as if you ran out of storage space.

- **Hobby equipment.** Sometimes sports and hobby equipment can multiply when you are not paying attention. Try leaving them in your car or arranged neatly in the garage to open up this space.

◆ **Light the way.** You know you need to have the back light working, but how about the switch for the backyard lights. Do they work? If buyers exit this door, can they see their way to their cars?

◆ **Mats and rugs.** Check the condition of your doormats. These rugs can be less formal and more rugged than your foyer rug. You can show function over style here.

The Least You Need to Know

◆ Impress buyers right away in the foyer so they fall in love with your home. Focus on the senses of sight and smell.

◆ Take photos of the views the buyers will first see. Change that view to make it the best you can. You want love at first sight.

◆ Unclutter the stairways to prevent accidents and give a spacious impression.

◆ End with a great impression of the back door area.

Chapter 9

The Living and Family Rooms

In This Chapter

- ◆ Decorating without a particular style
- ◆ Arranging for sight and traffic flow
- ◆ Inexpensive accessories that make the room
- ◆ Helping buyers see your home as a step up

Depending on the age of your home, you may have a living room, a family room, a great room, or a combination thereof. But the purpose is still the same—a room where the whole family gathers and spends much of its free time—where it lives. And since it is the first or second room most visitors see when entering the home, it sets the expectation for the entire property.

The living room is usually where the TV resides, along with a couch and some comfy chairs, as well as a fireplace, perhaps. Although newer homes may have both an informal living room, generally called the family room, and a living room, the more formal space where guests are entertained, we'll cover how to stage any and all of these spaces.

Minor Repairs

Because the living room is the hub of most family activities, it needs to be fully functional and ready to use. That means checking to be sure the major components are in top shape.

Fireplace

If you live in a climate where fireplaces are an important feature and your home has one, determine whether it can be used. Some mantles and fireplaces are decorative only and need to be described as such in any real estate listings. But if you have a working fireplace, make sure there are no obstructions, such as birds' nests, that have appeared since the last time you used it.

Of course, in some parts of the country, fireplaces may be of little use and relatively unimportant to buyers. But in northern climates, a fireplace can be a major draw. If that describes you, you'll want to be sure yours is in great shape—you'll get more money for your home if buyers can imagine their family snuggled around a crackling fire during snowy weather.

The furniture blocks the focal point of the room.

(Courtesy of Amy Ross and Beth Sammarone, The Redesign Team)

A no-cost furniture rear-rangement makes this room feel spacious.

(Courtesy of Amy Ross and Beth Sammarone, The Redesign Team)

Flooring

Because you see the floor more in the living room than anywhere else, it is important that it be in good shape. It doesn't matter whether it consists of wall-to-wall carpeting, hardwoods, or slate, as long as it looks like it can stand the test of time.

If the floor is not in great shape, you would be smart to invest in something new to freshen it up. Either a neutral area rug to cover all the marks on the hardwood floors or some inexpensive, but also neutral, wall-to-wall carpeting to replace the worn stuff you currently have down. You'll be amazed at how much nicer the room looks with new flooring in place.

Paint

Once again, neutral is the name of the game in paint for the living room, with cream, off-white, soft gold, and tan being the favored shades because anyone's furniture—no matter the style or color—will look good against these colors. If the room has woodwork that is stained, not painted, warmer tones will complement the wood and enhance this selling feature. But don't opt for bright white because it's too harsh and shows every conceivable defect.

Experts Explain

"We are selling your space, not your taste."

—Gina McNew, diva la difference interiors

Declutter and Clean

A living room is where most people spend their free time at home, but that doesn't mean that the room should serve multiple purposes. For instance, your treadmill should not be positioned in front of the TV, even if that's how you currently use it, nor should there be a model train running around the perimeter of the room, even if you're a huge model train fan.

Your goal in staging your living room is to show buyers how they could live there, not how you do. Hence, you need to clear out anything not specifically used in a living room, such as extra furniture that doesn't belong there, exercise equipment, or work files, to name a few.

Staging Snafu

While decluttering is a must in every room, don't go too far and take everything out. You still need books in the bookcases and mementos in the curio cabinet, for example, just not as many as you currently have.

Decluttering your living room entails removing any and all collections, whether they're golf trophies, sculptures, or family photos. Knick-knacks and mementos that distract buyers need to be packed up and removed from the room so that they can envision their own collections there.

This formal living room was taken over by toys.

(Courtesy of Nanette Catarinella, Room Styles Interiors)

With the toys gone, it appeals to a wider group of buyers.

(Courtesy of Nanette Catarinella, Room Styles Interiors)

As you're packing up your tchotchkes and collections, set aside anything bigger than a basketball to use in styling the room later. But anything smaller than your fist should be removed and packed away. Several smaller items look like clutter from a distance, since you can't always recognize what they are, while larger pieces provide a focal point.

Extra furniture that makes the room feel cramped, or doesn't coordinate with the main pieces you have, should also be taken out. The more that comes out, the more spacious the room will look and feel. Oversized furniture can have the same overpowering effect, making the room appear smaller, and should be dealt with the same way.

If you have a fireplace, you should remove any ashes and thoroughly sweep out the hearth. On the mantel, leave just one larger piece as a focal point, such as a nice vase or painting, but everything else that's up there should come down—photos, floral arrangements, greenery, candles, and anything else small. The key here is to draw attention to the fireplace, not your accessories. Any windows should be cleaned, inside and out, to increase the amount of outside light in the room, and window treatments steam cleaned.

Money Maker

One product we've found that is great at eliminating stubborn odors, especially in some upholstery, is Febreze. After you've steam cleaned, you might also apply a shot or two of Febreze before potential buyers come by, just as a little insurance against any lingering smells.

Steam cleaning is essential not just to get rid of dirt, but, more important, to get rid of odors. Next to the kitchen and bathrooms, the living room is where a lot of odors reside, because it's where you spend more of your time and because there are a lot of very absorbent fabrics in the room.

In addition to the drapes, you should plan on steam cleaning any upholstered pieces and carpeting to remove odors.

Furniture Placement

When staging your living room, you want to optimize the *sight lines* and traffic flow into the room.

def•i•ni•tion

A **sight line** is the view your eyes have of a room. If you can see everything in the room, the sight line is unobstructed, but if something gets in your way, such as a large plant or piece of furniture, your sight line is blocked.

That means arranging the furniture in such a way that visitors can get a clear view of everything in the room, including all the focal points and features.

Although furniture is usually clustered together to create cozy seating areas, when you're showing your home, you need it to be less functional and more maneuverable. Since there may be several groups checking out your home at once, such as during an open house, you need to place your furniture so that there is ample space for traffic flow—for people to walk around the room and not get stuck in a corner.

This diagram shows a typical living room with too much furniture.

(Software courtesy of Icovia, design courtesy of Julie Dana, The Home Stylist)

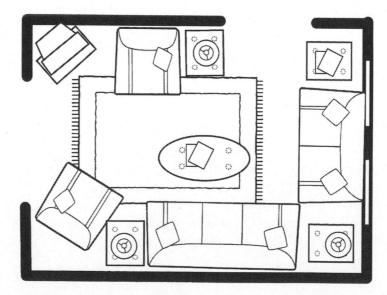

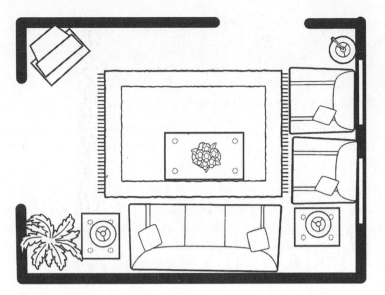

A simplified arrangement makes the room seem bigger.

(Software courtesy of Icovia, design courtesy of Julie Dana, The Home Stylist)

Floor Space

To maximize floor space, there should be none of the following on the floor:

◆ Baskets or magazine racks

◆ Decorative elements, such as duck decoys or animal statuettes

◆ Books

◆ Small plants, although large plants are okay

Removing as much as possible from the floor allows buyers to see the full extent of the space, which will seem larger if there are no items covering it. This is also the time to remove scatter or throw rugs. Large area rugs are okay unless they are covering hardwood floors, which are a desirable selling feature.

Lighting

To make the living area brighter, make sure you have at least three lamps, in addition to any overhead lighting. For instance, you may have two table lamps and one floor lamp in the room arranged in a triangle configuration in the room. That is,

Experts Explain

Lamps are the most commonly purchased items for staging.

you don't want all three clustered on one side of the room, or in one area—they need to be dispersed to spread the light evenly.

So that the lamps provide the maximum brightness possible, be sure you have the highest wattage light bulb allowable for the lamp base. Bulbs called daylight bulbs are a good choice because they give a more natural light to the space.

Lampshades should be white or off-white to allow maximum light to shine through. Darker shade colors, such as black, prevent the light from illuminating the space and enhancing the selling features.

In addition to adding light within the room, be sure you're not blocking any from coming in from the outside. That means potentially taking down any window treatments, blinds or sheers, especially if privacy isn't an issue. Removing anything blocking the window, such as a room air conditioner, is important. Also, pull back any drapes as far back to the side as possible, so that you see as much of the window as possible.

These heavy curtains are a dated look and they block light.

(Courtesy of Nanette Catarinella, Room Styles Interiors)

With curtains removed, this room feels bright and up-to-date.

(Courtesy of Nanette Catarinella, Room Styles Interiors)

Staging with Style

Of all the rooms in your home, the living room is where your style is defined, which means you have the greatest opportunity to capture a buyer's attention here.

If you have more than one living space, you'll want to differentiate the two so as not to confuse buyers. The following chart may help in determining how to accomplish that:

	Living Room	**Family Room**
Style	Formal	Casual
Who uses	Adults	Families
When	Company and special occasions	Friends and casual get-togethers
Staging accessories	Glossy magazines, like *Architectural Digest* A sculpture	A big Harry Potter book A board game in progress

If you only have one of these living areas, decorate the one room 80 percent like a living room and 20 percent like a family room. That means that it should be mainly formal, with a little playfulness to show that anyone can feel comfortable in it.

Decorating Tools

Making the most of your living space generally means removing some of what you currently have there, including extra pieces of furniture and lots of little accessories ("room dandruff" as TV interior decorating guru Christopher Lowell calls it).

Other things you'll definitely want to remove include ashtrays and evidence of food, such as chip and dip bowls or serving trays. Visitors don't like to see them out.

Money Maker

Placing high-end magazines out on the coffee table helps position your home as the step up buyers want. Those include *Vogue, Harvard Business Review, National Geographic,* and *Smithsonian,* for instance. But definitely not the *National Inquirer, Star, People,* and *First for Women,* which have a more low-brow reputation (although we still love them).

Bookcases should be an attractive feature in a room. In your bookcases, if you have any, you'll want to remove contents so that the cases are only 50 to 60 percent full when finished. Keep hardcover books, especially older ones, which give an air of sophistication to the room. If you have hardback books but they have dust jackets, just take the dust jackets off to make them appear older and more valuable. Remove all paperback books and family photos or memorabilia from the shelves.

Although there should only be one accessory on the fireplace mantel, a mirror is fine, too, because it reflects light into the room. You don't even have to hang it—you can set it on the mantel.

The room's focal point cannot be seen and the bookcase is disorganized.

(Courtesy of Amy Ross and Beth Sammarone, The Redesign Team)

Rearranging the furniture to see the fireplace makes the room appealing. The bookcase is also improved.

(Courtesy of Amy Ross and Beth Sammarone, The Redesign Team)

Any artwork in the room should be neutral and not taste-specific, such as contemporary or mixed media, for instance. Play it safe with landscapes and still life paintings that do not draw attention to themselves.

On the coffee table by the sofa, a *vignette* of larger items works well. However, there should only be a grouping of three. A sophisticated blend of a book, vase, and large two or three-wick candle is a nice selection, but don't feel you have to have that combination.

def•i•ni•tion

A **vignette** is a decorative grouping of accessories, usually in sets of three items. One is usually tall, one is medium height, and one is small, and they don't have to be the same. A clock, candle, and book, for example, could work well together.

To jazz up the living room without spending a lot of money, purchase a few accent pillows with a texture or pattern for the sofa and chairs. If the sofa is dated, consider slip covers or even draping it with a large painter's cloth and tuck it in for a clean and more up-to-date look. Roll magazines and push down between sofa back and cushions to keep slipcovers from slipping.

Two or three large plants in place in the living room are more than enough. One may be even better, depending on the size of the room.

The New Decorating Approach

Whether you're adding or subtracting pieces from your living room, you don't want to end up with a specific decorating style, such as cottage, southwestern, or mission, for example, unless it exactly matches the style of your home or the area. Decorating with a specific style in a more generic home is dangerous, because it's more likely that buyers won't like it than it is that they will. It's better to keep the style plain if the home's architecture does not dictate a particular style of decorating.

Money Maker

If you're staging a more casual family room, set out a board game to set the tone. But instead of Chutes and Ladders or Monopoly, aim for a little more sophistication, such as Stratego or Apples to Oranges.

The current look is clean lines with classic, but hip, accessories. Stick with a no frills approach with no dominant decorating style and you'll be safe. Again, remember your target market because what appeals to a 30-something may not appeal to a 60-something. Also, keep in mind that your accessories and props should befit the caliber of the home.

People considering buying a new home are typically looking to upgrade from their current home, which may be a starter house or apartment, for example. They want to feel that they're moving to a larger space with more flair. So you need to position your home as the step up socially that they're seeking. You can do that by aiming for a Pottery Barn look with upscale touches here and there.

The extra pillows on the couch make the room feel smaller and darker.

(Courtesy of Julie Dana, The Home Stylist)

The living room feels lighter and bigger with a simple classic look. The chess set adds a touch of class.

(Courtesy of Julie Dana, The Home Stylist)

The Least You Need to Know

- Don't try and decorate your living room, or your home, using a particular style—such as traditional or arts and crafts—unless the style of your home dictates it. Otherwise, a classic contemporary feel has the widest appeal.

- Since you see the floor the most in the living area, make sure it's in great shape.

- Because the living room is probably the most-used room in your home and it has the most fabric, it is also probably one of the smelliest, believe it or not. Steam clean all the fabric to try and get rid of any unwelcome scents.

- Look carefully through catalogs from companies like Pottery Barn, Storehouse, Restoration Hardware, Bombay, Pier 1, and Crate and Barrel to get a sense of what your room should look like in terms of amount of furniture and accessories. They will inspire you to create spaces that feel on-trend.

Chapter 10

The Dining Room

In This Chapter

- Reclaiming the dining room
- Minor repairs more than worth the money
- The ideal furniture arrangement
- Eye-catching styling secrets

The dining room is one of those rooms that can make quite an impression on buyers, despite the fact that it may be one of the least used rooms in the home—least used as it was intended, that is. Since dining rooms are often in the front of the home and are, therefore, one of the first rooms visitors see, they need to be stylish. That's where staging comes in.

After tackling any decluttering, cleaning, and minor repairs, we'll show you how to turn your ho-hum dining room into a showplace that will have buyers drooling.

Reclaim the Space

Through no fault of their own, dining rooms often become the catch-all room. Especially in homes with eat-in kitchens, dining rooms can become a space that is used for eating only at holidays. Not to mention the availability of a large horizontal surface—the table—which is perfect for piles to land on and stay there. With such infrequent use as a dining room, the purpose of such rooms has a tendency to morph into something else. Some of the most frequent alternate uses for a dining room include:

- Children's play area
- Home office
- Botanical garden
- Laundry folding area
- Exercise room
- Landing space for mail and miscellaneous belongings

Of course, when you decide to sell your home, one of your first orders of business is getting your dining room serving the purpose it is intended for, a dining room. That means clearing out everything that doesn't belong this room and packing it up or getting rid of it. The dining room should be nothing but a dining room.

In order to have the room feel as spacious as possible, the only furniture you should ultimately have in the room includes:

- A dining table and chairs
- A chandelier or light fixture
- One other piece, such as a china cabinet, sideboard, or buffet

Any more than this and the room will likely feel cramped.

The table does not match the color or style of the dining room.

(Courtesy of Kim Ausbury and Teresa Kratzer, Staged For You)

With a similar table, the dining room has a cohesive classic look.

(Courtesy of Kim Ausbury and Teresa Kratzer, Staged For You)

Whipping It Into Shape

As one of the first rooms buyers see when they enter your home, your dining room can make a statement that either impresses or disappoints. To make the most of the space, you'll want to pay close attention to any minor repairs that are needed, any clutter that needs removing, and any cleaning that needs to happen.

Repairs

As with any other room, you'll want to start at the top and work down. Check for any water spots on the ceiling, as well as any smoke damage, and paint over it to match the rest of the ceiling—better yet, paint the whole thing if you see spots that need covering. Spots of new paint are a sure give-away that there was something that needed attention.

Next, check to be sure your chandelier is working properly and that all the bulbs are functioning. Using the highest wattage bulbs allowed for that fixture will visually expand the space. There is usually a sticker inside the socket that tells you the maximum wattage recommended.

If your chandelier is obviously from another era or doesn't match the rest of your home, consider investing in a newer, more on-trend one. Always keep in mind the style of the home and do not try to mix a contemporary style with a Colonial home, or vice versa. Chandeliers do not have to be costly, remember we are going for a look more than anything else. If you love your chandelier and can't bear to part with it, now is the time to invest in a new one. You can take down the existing one and pack it up to move with you, as long as you buy a replacement to show with the home. But do not show your home with a chandelier you do not plan to leave.

Continuing down, the trim around any doorways should be painted and polished and any nicks repaired. Windows should be washed and the trim painted cream.

Money Maker

If you're painting over a very dark color, such as navy, brown, or burgundy, check into Kilz primer, which is a brand designed to cover dark colors with lighter ones.

This is one room where you can make a color statement. Use a color that is on-trend. Remember, an important aspect of staging is to neutralize it to make as appealing as possible to the largest number of buyers, but its goal is also to make it memorable. After all, buyers look at many homes, so you want yours to stand out. JoAnne Lenart-Weary of One Day Decorating calls this Signature Staging, in other words, something about the home should make it memorable to the potential buyers.

As you're prepping the walls for paint, check the switch plates and outlet covers to be sure you have them and that they're plain. If you're missing any, or if what you have features designs of any sort, invest in a set of switch plate and outlet covers in cream or to match the walls. You can install them once the paint is dry.

The best flooring in a dining room is hardwood, which should be cleaned. But if you have carpeting, you'll definitely want to clean it, too.

Declutter and Clean

After taking care of minor repairs, you'll want to tackle all the decluttering tasks covered in Chapter 4 and the cleaning steps outlined in Chapter 5. In the dining room, there are room specific projects to attend to. These projects include:

◆ Dusting and wiping off the chandelier and any individual shades or crystals

◆ Decluttering tops of any cabinets

- Clearing out the china cabinet and featuring one place setting per cabinet window opening

- Dusting and polishing the buffet

- Getting rid of any papers, clothing, and/or dying plants in the room—none of which belong there

Keeping the number of elements in the room to a minimum makes the dining room appear bigger. When buyers can't see the walls or the edges of the room it feels smaller to them, and smaller rooms lead to a smaller purchase offer.

Staging Snafu

Although green houseplants are a lovely accessory in any home, when you're staging your home to sell, you'll want to remove them from the tops of tall furniture, along with anything else that's sitting up there—vases, books, and any other accessories. Allowing buyers to see more space between the tops of furniture and the ceiling gives the illusion of a higher ceiling, and higher ceilings are worth money.

Arranging

Here are the key steps to staging your dining room for maximum effect:

- Table—take out all extra leaves in the dining room table, to make it as small as possible.

- Table location—the table should be in the center of the room, directly under the chandelier.

- Chairs—four chairs is an ideal number, but up to six is okay. No more than six though, or the room will look crowded.

- Spacing—buyers should be able to walk around the table easily.

- Chandelier—should be centered over the table and set 34" to 36" above the table top.

- Rug—a rug underneath the table is recommended, especially if you have hardwood floors, but the size of the rug required varies according to the size of the table.

*To determine the appropri-
ate rug size for your dining
room, pull out a chair as if
you were going to sit down.
Now measure the length and
width from chair to chair.
Then add one foot to each
measurement to get the correct length and width.*

*(Software courtesy of Icovia,
design courtesy of Julie Dana,
The Home Stylist)*

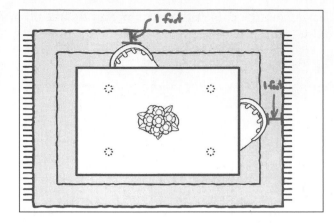

Brightening

Having a bright, cheerful dining room is important to buyers, who will imagine spending holidays with their families there. You want to create a happy impression, and lighting helps.

Start by checking to be sure all the lights in the room have the maximum bulb capacity—the highest wattage.

If you have windows with curtains on them, push the curtains as far to the sides as possible, to let the sunlight in. If you have blinds, pull them all the way up, so they don't block the window view. Or take them down entirely—it's more important to have as much light as possible filtering in than to show off your window treatments.

If the room is still a little dark, bring in extra lamps. Make sure they are tall accent lamps, for use on buffet tables, for instance, rather than table lamps, which are much bigger and bulkier. You don't want buyers to notice the lamps themselves, just how bright the room is.

Also, be sure there are no electrical cords to trip over as buyers walk around the room—either use extension cords to be able to keep cords against the wall and out of the walkway or relocate lights so that cords are not an issue.

Stylish Eating

Making your dining room even more attractive comes down to some well-known staging tricks, all of which you can do yourself. If you don't have a separate dining room, or you have a room and no furniture for it, we'll share some ideas for convert-ing available components into traditional dining room furniture.

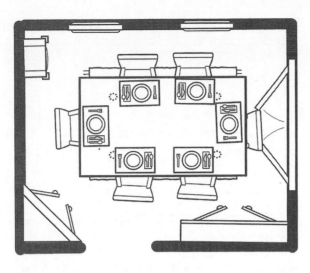

This is how a dining room is typically arranged, with buffets, china cabinet and grandfather clock in place.

(Software courtesy of Icovia, design courtesy of Julie Dana, The Home Stylist)

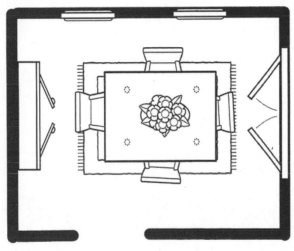

By removing a table leaf and two chairs, leaving one buffet and a nice centerpiece, you can see how much larger and pleasing to the eye the room is.

(Software courtesy of Icovia, design courtesy of Julie Dana, The Home Stylist)

Styling a China Cabinet

Besides a table and chairs, the other large piece of furniture in the dining room is typically a china cabinet with a glass front. Terrific storage units and beautiful pieces, china cabinets can be stunning. But they need to be staged properly or they can look like a junk collection.

Most people center their displays on each shelf of the china cabinet, forgetting that it gets split in two when the door is closed. A better method is to style one side, then the other.

On each shelf, there should be no more than three items on each side, clustered with the tallest piece in back and two shorter pieces in front of it.

Staging Secrets

Once the basic rearranging and fixing has been accomplished, it's time to start decorating and staging the dining room for buyers. Here are some do's and don'ts to getting a favorable reaction from buyers.

The following is a list of Do's:

♦ If your table is in good condition, use a table runner OR place mats at each place to show off the wood; don't use both and don't use tablecloths.

♦ Do spend some money on a nice bouquet of fresh flowers before an open house or showing. Use it as a dining room table centerpiece. Stick with a petite bunch, however, not a huge monstrosity, so that buyers won't be distracted from looking at the room itself.

♦ Do hang artwork with a generic landscape, a food motif, or a mirror in the room.

♦ Do pack up your collections of pretty tea cups and saucers

The following is a list of Don'ts:

♦ In the center of the table, don't have salt and pepper shakers or condiments sitting out.

♦ Don't set the table for a meal—it looks too fake. You can put a *charger* at each setting with a napkin in the center with a napkin ring.

def•i•ni•tion

A **charger** is essentially a decorative plate that you set your dinner plate on. They come in solid colors, generally metallic.

♦ Don't display valuables like your grandmother's silver tea set or an expensive vase for fear that an unscrupulous visitor will walk off with it, or try and come back later for it.

♦ Don't let anyone see any liquor, including wine. Some folks may be offended, so don't take the chance. Stow it away.

This dining room is over-accessorized with lace tablecloths and window treatments, not to mention the abundance of furniture.

(Courtesy of Julie Dana, The Home Stylist)

Pushing the curtains back, removing some of the lace, and taking out some of the furniture makes this room feel much brighter and bigger.

(Courtesy of Julie Dana, The Home Stylist)

What makes the biggest positive impression on buyers is a minimal amount of appropriate furniture and a beautiful bouquet. Let the dining room shine on its own, without the distractions of lots of accessories.

Staging Snafu

Unless every other home in your neighborhood has crown molding or a chair rail in their dining room, there is little to be gained by adding one now. They force you to line up furniture symmetrically in the room and not all buyers will like the style. If the room is small and has chair rail, consider removing it as it will visually enlarge the space.

If You Don't Have a Dining Room

If you don't have a separate dining room, you'll need to have a sit down eating area somewhere in your home. Fortunately, it's not hard to create.

One option is to set up a small ice cream parlor table and set of two chairs up in a little corner, such as in the kitchen, at the end of the living room, or near the kitchen.

Even if it's part of another room, treat the dining space as if it is its own room. Dress up the table like a formal dining room, complete with floral centerpiece. Pull back curtains to let in light and set a couple of chargers down with napkins to set the mood.

On the other hand, if you have a dining room but no table, here are some ideas for creating one:

◆ Use a pair of sawhorses and a door. Throw a tablecloth over it and set chairs around it and no one will ever know.

◆ Bring an indoor/outdoor plastic table from outside in with a tablecloth that covers all the way to the floor.

◆ Cinder blocks and a piece of wood can also work. And a king size sheet can also work as a tablecloth in a pinch.

Staging Snafu

Wallpaper borders at or near the top of the walls were very popular for quite sometime, but not anymore. Not only do borders make your home feel out of date, they also make the ceiling feel lower, neither of which you want.

Really, any rectangular shape will work as long as you cover it.

The Least You Need to Know

◆ Even if your dining room is currently functioning as a work out room, children's play area, or dumping ground for paper, you need to convert it back to a dining room for buyers.

◆ Having too many pieces of furniture in a dining room can make it appear way too small. A table with no leaves in it, four chairs, and a buffet or cabinet is all that should be in the room.

◆ Make sure you have the maximum light possible in the room by pulling back curtains as far as they will go, putting the maximum wattage light bulbs in all the fixtures, and adding tall accent lights if needed.

◆ Remove anything from the tops of bookshelves or cabinets, such as vases, books, or plants, which can make the room seem shorter than it is.

◆ Don't add crown molding or a chair rail unless all the other homes in your neighborhood—your comparables to which your property will be compared—have them. Otherwise, they won't be worth the time and money.

Chapter 11

The Kitchen

In This Chapter

- Freshening your kitchen
- Where to spend your time and money
- A shopping list of essential elements
- Making the best first impression

Your kitchen is the heart of your home—the most important room to buyers and the one that can make or break a sale. For that reason, it's the most valuable room of all.

While the kitchen's main purpose is food preparation, its role has expanded considerably in the last few decades. In addition to cooking meals, homeowners now entertain, pay bills, and watch TV in their kitchen, among other things. For that reason, it probably gets more usage than other rooms.

Of course, rooms that are used more may also be in greater need of staging help.

Minor Repairs

In the best of all possible worlds, buyers want to see a kitchen that is spacious, bright, updated, neutral, and clean—with an emphasis on clean.

To fulfill the desire for a kitchen that is move-in ready, you may find you need to do some minor repairs to fix areas that have become broken or rundown, or replace some components that are showing their age, such as an orange hued countertop or worn avocado colored linoleum flooring.

> ### Experts Explain
>
> When a real estate agent calls to tell you they are on their way over to show your home to a potential buyer, the best use of the next 10 or 15 minutes is cleaning the kitchen. Don't worry as much about clutter or other areas of the home. Focus instead on making your kitchen as appealing as you can in the time you have.

Tiles

If you have tiles on your counter or backsplash that are broken or have stained grout, now is the time to replace and regrout.

Remove any tiles that are chipped or cracked and replace them with matching ones that you have purchased. Or if your grout is stained or doesn't match due to repairs through the years, you'll want to take up the tile and redo it with a fresh coat of grout. You'll be amazed at what a difference new tile and grout will make in the kitchen.

Stove Hood

If you have a hood over your stove for venting, consider replacing it. A shiny, new hood is worth far more to buyers than the $100 or so it will cost to buy a new one. However, if you really don't want to spend the money, take it off and remove the grease and grime completely. It's relatively easy to take off and on, but the degreasing may be time-consuming.

Countertop

In the kitchen, countertops are perhaps the most important feature. So if you are debating where to invest any money, put it into new countertops. In fact, if you can only do one thing to your home, consider replacing worn or outdated countertops—you'll get the biggest impact from the change, both in terms of appearance and your purchase price.

The size of this kitchen cannot be appreciated because of the distractions.

(Courtesy of Amy Ross and Beth Sammarone of The Redesign Team)

The removal of items helps to show of the kitchen's spaciousness.

(Courtesy of Amy Ross and Beth Sammarone of The Redesign Team)

If your countertops are a neutral color—beige, cream, light grey, soft gold—and are in good condition—no stains or excessive wear—all you really need to do is clean them. Take a look at the laminate edge, however, and if it is coming off, reglue and clamp it.

However, if the countertops are a non-neutral color, such as forest green or country blue, which were extremely popular in decades past, you'll want to make some changes. Keep in mind, however, that the countertop should be commensurate with the caliber of the house. If most of the comparable homes feature granite or Corian, then you should consider updating your countertops to be at the same quality level.

Experts Explain

"Set the proper stage by remembering your target market. Who are you staging for? If your target market is young families, then you need more of a Pottery Barn look. If your target market is older, than you would go for more of a Horchow or Bombay look."

—JoAnne Lenart-Weary of One Day Decorating

The first option is to paint the countertops, being very careful to select a proper primer and neutral paint color. This is probably the least expensive way to change the total look of the counter and the room.

Another option is to tile over the top of the counters, which you'd probably only want to consider if you have a laminate surface. Matching the grout to the tile color is recommended these days, so take that into account when you're making the purchase.

Money Maker

Before an open house or buyer tour, make sure your real estate agent is familiar with all the hidden gems in your home. Point out where the light switch is for the under-the-counter lights, for instance, or show them where the hidden spice rack is in the cupboards. Your agent should be made aware of all the little touches that make your home better than similar homes in the area.

Even if you tile just the island, if you have one, the transformation of that one dominant fixture can upgrade the entire kitchen's appearance.

If those aren't options you want to explore, replacing the countertops with neutral colored surfaces is smart.

Don't forget, depending on what's standard in your neighborhood, you might want to replace it with another laminate countertop, or you might see that Corian, granite, or marble is expected and will help show your home is worth more than other homes in the area.

Flooring

Another area where you can make changes that have a big impact on your kitchen's perceived value is the floor.

If your linoleum flooring is worn or outdated, it's a fairly easy do-it-yourself job to use peel-and-stick tiles to cover up what's there. Of course, having the linoleum pulled up and replaced is another more expensive way to go, but if you're doing it yourself, consider the peel-and-stick method.

When choosing new linoleum, you want to get the most expensive looking you can find. Today that means marble-looking or variegated shades that resemble stone, with neutral colors. Don't go with solid bright white, however, because dirt is extremely obvious—light-colored neutral tones are best.

If you have hardwood floors, having them stripped and resealed can boost their appearance and value to the buyer, who doesn't have to add floor stripping to their list of things to do after they move in.

Do not use any throw or scatter rugs even in front of a sink or stove. It will visually shrink the space.

And if you have tile, you'll want to replace any that are damaged and regrout them if the color is not consistent throughout the room. If you replace the tile, go for the largest tile that will fit well in the space and, if possible, lay in on the diagonal to make the room feel larger.

Money Maker

If you have a busy linoleum pattern that you can't replace or cover, buy a bound neutral rug to cover most of the floor. Having a large solid-colored light tan rug in the room will dampen the effect of any outdated colors and shapes, for very little money.

Walls

Neutral colored painted walls are your goal in the kitchen, so buyers can picture living there, rather than be distracted by your decorating style—which is unlikely to be exactly like theirs.

That's especially true when it comes to wallpaper—wallpaper is very taste specific and it would be surprising, really, if you found many buyers who like the pattern you chose for your kitchen walls. That includes any borders, too.

Borders and wallpaper can be great to express your style and personality in your home, but when you're trying to help buyers envision their furniture and personal style in your rooms, you don't want to make it more difficult. A warm, neutral palette is best.

Although it can be time-consuming, removing wallpaper isn't tough. If you rent a steamer, the job will go even faster. But be assured it will be worth the time and effort. Taking down borders and wallpaper will brighten the room, update it—especially if the wallpaper has been up for a while—and make it feel more spacious. Another option for removing paper is to score it with a product like Paper Tiger and then spray it with two-thirds warm water and one-third vinegar. Let it sit for a few minutes and then scrape off with wide putty blade.

Lighting

Any light fixtures you have in the kitchen, from hanging lamps and chandeliers over the kitchen table or island to wall sconces, should be free of color and decorating motif. That means no red trim around the edges or roosters on the dome, because potential buyers may have a love of ultra modern style, or may see red as bad luck. You just never know.

Fortunately, replacing light fixtures does not have to be an expensive proposition. Usually with $100 to $200, you can update your kitchen by several years.

Staging Snafu _____

If your kitchen has a large rectangular fluorescent fixture overhead, it's generally not worth it to replace it. Granted, it may be a little out-of-date, but you won't recoup your investment if you decide now to replace it with something else. Save your money.

Declutter and Clean

Remember that the kitchen's primary function is food preparation, so begin your staging of the room by removing or relocating anything that doesn't have to do with food and cooking. That includes the kids' homework papers, bills, medication, the calendar, photos, etc. Also collections you may have displayed there, such as salt and pepper shakers or teacups and saucers, should come down and be packed away.

When buyers see things other than pots and pans, dishes, and food in a kitchen, they assume that there simply isn't enough storage space elsewhere in the home, and that's a big negative. You want buyers to feel that they are moving up to your home—getting more space or maybe moving to a nicer neighborhood—and that there is plenty of room to grow into. The last thing you want them to worry about is the size of the kitchen.

Once you've cleared off countertops and filed away important papers or special artwork, you can start to clean and brighten the room.

Sink

First, the basics. If you have any dirty dishes in the sink or strainer, clean them or dry them and put them away. Although washing dishes is a daily necessity for us all, buyers don't want to be reminded of work. The lack of any kind of evident housework implies that your home is so easy to take care of, they won't be spending lots of time on upkeep.

After you've cleared out the sink and cleaned it so it sparkles, put away any cleaning devices, such as sponges, cleaning sprays, and powders.

Refrigerator and Appliances

As the largest appliance in your kitchen, the refrigerator attracts a lot of attention. To be sure it makes the best impression, clear the front of any magnets, papers, artwork, photos, calendars, and anything else you may have attached there. Then use a cleaning spray to wipe it down so it shines and removes those pesky fingerprints.

Make sure that other appliances look clean, in good working order. Again, this is a place where the quality and caliber of the appliances should be in keeping with the price of the house.

The kitchen is a naturally cluttered space and an empty surface, like the front of the refrigerator, is an inviting place for your eye to rest.

If you have to hang your calendar in the kitchen, some other options—besides the refrigerator door—are the side of the refrigerator or the inside of a cupboard door, out of sight.

This may be how you nor-mally keep the front of your refrigerator.

(Courtesy of Julie Dana, The Home Stylist)

By clearing off the front of the largest appliance, it make the kitchen feel larger and cleaner.

(Courtesy of Julie Dana, The Home Stylist)

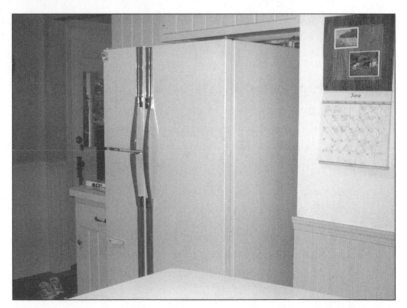

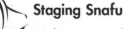

Staging Snafu _____

Make sure any liquor or empty cans and bottles are out of sight so as not to offend anyone, or to suggest that you drink more than you do. So if you have beer can recyclables sitting out that you've been meaning to return for ages, now would be a good time.

Trashcan

Another item you don't want out in the open is a trashcan. No one wants to see or, worse, smell your garbage, so make sure your trashcan is empty and cleaned out before any buyers stop by. Freshening it by scouring the inside of the can with a product like Pine Sol will get rid of lingering odors and will suggest to any visitors that you regularly keep your kitchen in tip top shape. Put your trashcan under the sink, in a closet, or in an under-the-counter cupboard. If it simply won't fit anywhere else, keep it in the room but make sure it has a lid so that no one can see the contents.

Countertops

Although your counters are now new or updated, they still need to be decluttered and cleaned. After wiping counters down, remove everything from the surface and either pack it away or store it in a cupboard or closet. Then put three items out—no more, no less—to help buyers imagine what it would be like to live in your home and use your kitchen. The three items might include a coffee pot, toaster oven, and canisters, for example. But more than that will clutter the counters and make them appear less spacious.

The kitchen counter appears small because of excessive appliances and cooking items.

(Courtesy of Julie Dana, The Home Stylist)

Clearing the countertops of clutter makes the whole kitchen seem bigger and brighter.

(Courtesy of Julie Dana, The Home Stylist)

Hanging Rack and Tools

If you have a hanging pot rack in your kitchen, perhaps over a central island or stove top, you'll want to take it down.

Hanging racks are an excellent way to gain easy access to pots and pans without taking up cupboard space, but when selling your home, they act as a clunky curtain, blocking the view into the room or into other rooms beyond the kitchen. In a word, hanging racks add clutter, which is the last thing you want in the most important room in your home.

If you have hanging cooking utensils, spice racks or knife blocks, it is best to take them down. You want a spacious uncluttered look.

Adding Style

The one word you want buyers to use to describe your kitchen is "fresh." Keep that in mind as you clean and accessorize.

Staging Snafu _____

Contrary to popular advice, don't bake cookies or bread during a house tour. Baked goods have a strong aroma that can be overpowering to buyers. It also makes them wonder what odors you may be trying to cover up. A better approach to freshening the air is to open all your windows for 10 or 15 minutes.

To Be Purchased

Some kitchen accessory essentials are:

♦ New placemats and coordinating napkins for the table

♦ New dishtowels

♦ Bowl of fresh fruit, such as lemons, or fresh flowers, placed on the island or on the kitchen table

That doesn't mean you need to spend lots of money, but, as always, get pieces that look more expensive than they are. One of the best places to find such items is your local dollar store. And if you have a garden, or a neighbor with a garden, head there for some fresh flowers.

To Remove

If you have a window in the kitchen with a window treatment on it, take the curtain or valence down. The main reason is to let as much light into the room as possible, but since cooking areas tend to get pretty greasy, taking the curtain down also removes a potentially greasy accessory. Remember to clean the windows inside and out.

If you have an island in your kitchen, you'll also want to be sure to remove everything from the surface and clean it thoroughly. Then keep the surface totally clear, except for the bowl of fresh fruit or vase of fresh flowers we mentioned.

 Money Maker _____

If you have more than one eating area, such as a dining room and an eat-in kitchen or kitchen countertop, style the dining room table more formally than the kitchen eating area. In the dining room, use a table runner or tablecloth on the table, and in the kitchen use placemats and more casual napkins.

This represents a typical busy decorating message in a kitchen. The busy wallpaper is not a selling point.

(Courtesy of Kim Ausbury and Teresa Kratzer, Staged For You)

Now the kitchen almost looks ready for buyers. The next step is to remove the remaining wallpaper.

(Courtesy of Kim Ausbury and Teresa Kratzer, Staged For You)

Islands are very noticeable and anything on the top will make the room appear cluttered.

Animal dishes are another item to be removed, or at least moved, during buyer tours. Consider where buyers are likely to want to walk and move any water and food bowls out of the high traffic areas. The best solution is to pick them up and store them in your car when the house is on tour. This is important for a variety of reasons.

The perception for many people, even animal lovers, is that pets make a house dirty. Also, for those with a fear of animals, the evidence of pets may make them uncomfortable to view the house not knowing if the pets are lurking around the corner.

The same goes for cat litter boxes—move them elsewhere, such as the basement or garage—after cleaning them carefully. If you relocate a stinky box, it will only serve to stink up a different room of your home, but if you move a clean box, it's less offensive to those who come into your home.

The Least You Need to Know

- The kitchen can make or break a home sale. The condition and appearance of a kitchen, where buyers expect to spend a lot of time, weighs heavily in a purchase decision.

- Countertops are the most important element in a kitchen and should be as up-to-date and cleared of clutter as possible. If you can do only one thing in the whole home, consider replacing outdated countertops with neutral new ones, or painting over what you have.

- Add a bowl of fresh fruit or a vase of fresh flowers to have buyers thinking "fresh" thoughts while they tour your kitchen. Fresh and clean are the watchwords to shoot for.

- Because it's one of the most dominant surfaces in your kitchen, make sure the front of your refrigerator is totally clear of any notes, pictures, calendars, and magnets, and wiped clear of fingerprints.

Chapter **12**

The Bedrooms

In This Chapter

- ◆ Minor repairs for major impact
- ◆ Are you sure it is ready for inspection?
- ◆ Making bedrooms spacious and bright
- ◆ Styling bedrooms to make a positive impression

Bedrooms are very private places. Even good friends and family rarely spend time in your master bedroom, and now you are letting strangers explore this private domain. Bedrooms, ranging from master suites to baby nurseries, can impact how comfortable buyers feel in your home and ultimately how comfortable they are with putting in an offer. By depersonalizing this private space and emphasizing a luxurious feeling, you can make buyers feel at home and ready to buy.

Focus on Buyer's Goals, Not Yours

To sell your home for its maximum value, you need to re-focus on the sole purpose of each room, in this case, the bedroom.

Purpose of the Bedroom

Children's bedrooms are for sleeping, relaxing, playing, and studying. Master bedrooms are for sleeping, relaxing, reading, and, well, let's also call it playing. Master bedrooms are not for—at least in the eyes of the buyer—folding laundry, exercising, ironing, working, or storing junk that doesn't fit in any other room. And children's room are not gymnasiums or toy stores, despite the fact that they may currently look like one.

Bedrooms are such an inner sanctuary, so private, that we are comfortable letting them get a little messy, and maybe a little cluttered. Public rooms, like the living room, we usually clean and tidy up when company is coming, but many times even diligent homeowners will let the bedrooms slide.

Maybe you like your exercise equipment in there so you are reminded first thing in the morning of what you should be doing—like hanging up the clothes that got draped across the equipment—or really working up a sweat. Or maybe you're a doctor with medical texts nearby in order to accurately answer a late night emergency call. Many of us consider our bedrooms multi-purpose rooms, but buyers see them only as relaxation areas, so you need to give them what they want.

The Focal Point of the Bedroom

The focal point of the bedroom should be the bed. This may seem obvious, but in many bedrooms, children's in particular, the bed is barely noticeable. Typically, other furniture, toys, or accessories, dominate the room. However, in all cases, the bed should be the dominant piece of furniture in the room—easily visible from the doorway.

This child's room is a little too wild for buyers to see its potential.

(Courtesy of Nanette Catarinella, Room Styles Interiors)

The spaciousness of the room can now be appreciated—and it's still cute.

(Courtesy of Nanette Catarinella, Room Styles Interiors)

Experts Explain

"Remember, the elimination of personal tastes, strong colors, and posters, pictures, or other accessories that may distract or even be offensive makes it easier for buyers to imagine themselves living there"

—Martha Webb, author of *Dress Your House for Success: 5 Fast, Easy Steps to Selling your House, Apartment or Condo for the Highest Possible Price*

In a master bedroom, having a full or queen-sized bed is optimal, although a king-sized bed will work if the room is large enough. What doesn't work so well is two twin beds, a la the old Desi and Lucy TV show. It is difficult for buyers to visualize whether a larger bed will fit in the space. Two twin beds also make it hard to determine which bedroom of the several in this home is the master bedroom. This may seem silly, but twin beds in a master bedroom can confuse buyers, and confused buyers don't buy homes.

Remember the potential buyer is looking for a dream … the dream of a perfect life that a new home may bring them. Perhaps this thought process is not realistic but it is a human instinct. Master bedrooms should reflect the idea of a perfect relationship. When accessorizing this room use matching pairs in a variety of ways such as lamps, throw pillows, pair of chairs in a seating area. This will send the message of a strong relationship.

Other Furniture

In a master bedroom, if there is extra space, you might have a sitting area, consisting of two chairs and table, for reading and relaxing.

Bedrooms can, and generally do, also have dressers and night stands. Secondary bedrooms, such as the kids' rooms or guest rooms, can also have dressers and sometimes a desk, but they should be neat and tidy—your kids can pretend that is where they do their homework.

As a general rule, anything with a nonsleeping/relaxing purpose should not be in the bedrooms. Having other recreational items or storage such as a makeshift gym locker, recording studio, science lab, or replicas of the space shuttle can distract buyers and make the actual size and shape of the room seem smaller.

Money Maker

Have clothes hampers with lids in each bedroom. Hampers help to keep clothes contained, but in a pinch (last minute showing), you can toss clutter into them.

When there are a lot of extra items in the bedroom, the buyer might also think that there must not be much room in the home—if there were storage, they would assume you'd be putting more things away there. But because you haven't, storage must be lacking—this is what they'll think.

For buyers, the purpose of looking at the bedrooms is to see if they will meet their needs. However, you need to keep in mind that the demographic of the family may be different from yours and their needs may be different. For instance, you might have school-age children and their children might be grown and out of the home. Or perhaps you're retired and some potential buyers might be single professionals. You can't assume everyone who looks at your home will be like you, so you need to stage the bedrooms, and other rooms, to help anyone envision themselves living there.

Bedroom Staging Example

Let's say you are a married couple with two small sons. Your sons' bedrooms are chock full of action heroes, Legos, and Hot Wheels tracks. Your master bedroom has a bed, but also a treadmill in one corner and a cluttered but useful computer desk in the other.

Now let's say the first family to look at your home is a divorced mom with two teenage girls. This group will have a hard time looking past the blue and green colors in the kids' rooms and the exercise bike that reminds the mom she can never find enough time to exercise. She doesn't even want to think about having to repaint two bedrooms pink and purple. She says "no thanks."

In staging these bedrooms, there are number of things you can do to make it appealing to the largest number of buyers. First, you could remove the exercise equipment and slide the computer desk into the closet. The boys' rooms you paint cream. Then the same potential buyers might react differently: "This master bedroom feels like the sanctuary I so desperately need, and the girls can decorate their rooms and everything will look nice. Or maybe over the summer we can paint the room, but we don't have to do it immediately. This home is perfect for us."

Or let's say the second people who look at the home are a mature couple who want the secondary bedrooms as home offices for each of them. They look at your two neutral secondary bedrooms and say: "We can set up our offices the day we move in. This home is perfect for us."

By keeping the rooms neutral in color and sparse in décor, you've allowed buyers with very different needs to envision their own things in the home. And now you have two parties very interested in your home, which brings a smile to your face because of the anticipated bidding war sure to ensue.

Selling the Bedroom

The goals for the master bedroom are two-fold: to make the bed the focal point and for it to feel like a beautiful sanctuary that anyone will feel comfortable and relaxed in.

The goals for the secondary bedrooms can be a little tricky, but with guidance from this book, you can do it.

Secondary rooms should be as gender-neutral as possible. The less a room designates that a specific gender lives there, the easier it is to show other families that their children can settle right in. This doesn't mean it is a boring, generic guest bedroom, but it can't have a dominant "boy theme," such as Spiderman or fire engines, or a dominant "girl theme," such as ballerinas and princesses.

> **Staging Snafu**
>
> Do not assume that buyers won't go through bedside drawers or take a quick look in your closet. For that reason, keep personal marital aids tucked away. A surprising number of couples leave them out in the open, to the embarrassment of all in the room when they are discovered.

It should also be difficult to determine the exact age of the child who lives in a secondary bedroom. The buyer will probably be able to tell if this is a toddler's room or a teenager's room, but the more inviting it is to all ages, the easier buyers can imagine their own children living there. So by simply rolling up your teenager's rock band posters, or packing away the no-longer-used diaper changing table, it helps to de-emphasize the occupant's age and make buyers feel it will meet their needs, whatever the age of their own children.

Making Minor Repairs

Nothing ruins the feeling of tranquility in a master bedroom quicker than things needing repair. It's time for a honey-do list. Maybe you'll be the honey that does the repairing, or maybe you'll hire someone to get the job done. Regardless, here are some minor repair hot spots for you to check. Because you have lived in the home for so long, sometimes it is easy to remember how things used to be, not, in fact, how they really look now, which is why it's important to personally look at each item:

- **Lighting.** Make sure all light bulbs work and are the highest wattage permitted by the lamp manufacturer.

- **Windows.** Check that none of the windows has a crack in the pane. Remove any plastic covering used to block drafts.

- **Doors.** Do all the doors easily open and shut?

- **Ceiling fans.** If you have one, does it squeak and wobble? Have you gotten up there to dust it recently?

- **Art work.** Have you removed all personal family photographs and posters? Have you patched the holes from the pictures that used to hang there?

- **Wall color.** Are all bedrooms a neutral cream paint color? This includes the secondary bedrooms, too. This also means no paneling or wallpaper. Yes, we understand that taking down wall paper is an absolute pain, but taking down wallpaper is necessary in all rooms of your home if you want to get the maximum selling price.

- **Floors.** Do the carpets need a good steam cleaning? Should the rug be replaced?

Money Maker

You want to choose restful and peaceful colors for bedrooms. For staging, you do not want a bold or vibrant color, such as red. The first color choice for staging is cream, but other colors that also work well are creamy soft yellow, light taupe, or very muted sage green.

*With cleaning and declutter-
ing done, this bedroom now
lacks a personality.*

*(Courtesy of Julie Dana, The
Home Stylist)*

*Adding simple pictures and
patterned pillows helps to
give the room punch.*

*(Courtesy of Julie Dana, The
Home Stylist)*

By fixing these minor trouble spots, potential buyers will feel relaxed. The bedroom,
more than any other room in the home, should be a relaxing carefree place for buyers.

Declutter and Clean

By now you know that a thoroughly clean home is important to attracting buyers.
There are several specific things you can do in your master and secondary bedrooms
to emphasize how clean and fresh they are.

It is helpful to wash all the bedding. Washing the comforters, pillow shams, bed skirts, as well as the sheets will freshen the room by sight and with the slight fresh fragrance of detergent, which suggests, "clean." If bedding needs replaced go for neutrals or that posh hotel kind of look with a down comforter folded across the bottom of the bed. Use the best quality of linens you can afford to give a look of quality. Add some throw pillows for interest but do not overdo this decorator look.

Washing the windows helps ensure the view will really be appreciated. Throw your curtains in the wash, too, if you can. How about those blinds? Are they dusty?

Horizontal surfaces in particular collect dust quickly. Have you checked under the bed for dust bunnies? Oh, under the bed is crammed full of stuff? Maybe it is time to clean that out, too. Buyers will look everywhere, including under your bed. Any possessions under there can signal to buyers that there is not enough storage space in the home.

Money Maker

If you are struggling for storage in your bedroom, try stashing off-season clothes in empty suitcases. Or move a tall dresser into the walk-in to free up floor space in the room.

Because you see your nightstand and dresser everyday, it is easy not to really notice them any more. Take a good look at the dressers in your room and the secondary rooms. Do they need to be tidied and dusted? Buyers like to see tidy dressers.

While you are doing the final declutter and cleaning checks, be sure to notice if there are any valuables out in the open. You do not want to have jewelry boxes sitting on the dressers. It is too bad that it needs to be mentioned, but some folks can't be trusted, so remove the temptation. This includes the "change jar" and the gold watch on the nightstand.

Take another look at the top of the master bedroom dresser.

Remove personal elements such as deodorant, or a big messy pile of necklaces, or even a group of dusty perfume bottles. This clutter makes buyers feel like they are invading your personal space. Making it less personal and less cluttered helps buyers relax.

The last thing to do is to plant the subliminal message that this home requires no work to keep it clean. You may think this is awfully silly, because we all know that no matter where we move, there will be laundry and dirty clothes. But reminding people that they will need to do housework, and especially seeing other people's dirty clothes, even if in a laundry basket, does not help to sell the home.

Making It Light and Spacious

As you know, normally you want your bedroom dim for sleeping (or maybe romance), but when you sell your home you want to show buyers it is light and bright—just the opposite of how you normally like to live. For buyers, bright and light equals space, and space equals a dream home.

What's the Wattage?

The amount of light in a room helps the room seem much bigger than it is. Just about everyone's bedroom lacks adequate lighting.

If you have an overhead light, now is the time to check if all the light bulbs are in there and are the highest wattage allowed by the socket. Do the same for the night-stand lights and any lights on your dressers.

An inexpensive trick for making the room brighter is changing the shade on the lamp. Even the best of us can have trouble getting the dust off lampshades and some-times they are yellowed and cracked. Purchasing new lampshades in white or light cream can dramatically lighten the room for very little money.

Another way to make the room seem brighter, and therefore, more spacious, is to make sure the curtains are pulled away from the window. Push them far to each side or completely remove them to show the most amount of window you can. If your curtains are currently tied back remove the tie-backs to give them a more on-trend look.

Money Maker

When staging the bedroom, you want a balanced, symmetrical look. Sometimes you don't have two matching lamps for each side of the bed, but don't waste money purchasing new lamps. Instead just get new matching shades and place a hardcover book or two under the shorter lamp. The two lamps will appear uniform.

While at the windows, have you really looked at your blinds or shades lately? It is so easy for them to get dusty, and maybe a little dingy. They get dusty even in the most meticulously clean home, so don't take it as a sign of poor housekeeping. But now that you are selling your home, we want to be able to satisfy even the most nit-picky person. By removing the dust on the blinds or shades and washing the windows, more of that soothing sunshine can shine in.

Remember to go through the same process in secondary bedrooms—replacing bulbs with higher wattage varieties, pulling back or removing curtains, and cleaning blinds and anything on the windows.

Make It Look Spacious

In addition to adding light, there are a few other things you can do to show buyers how spacious all your bedrooms are.

First, look at the amount of furniture in the room. Is all the furniture lined up against all the walls? Buyers look specifically at the size of the bedrooms. Do you know how to show off the size? It is simple. Make sure you can see all four corners of the room. To do this you may have to place the bed so it juts out into the room perpendicular to the wall.

Making it look as spacious as possible may also include removing some furniture from the room. This could include the extra bookcase or extra dresser. Extra furniture, even though you may need it to live in the room, should be removed to show off the room to buyers. When you remove the extra dresser, it becomes a great piece to store off-season clothes and other nonessentials in its new place in the basement or in off-site storage.

This bedroom is classic yet stale.

(Courtesy of Carie Baumann, Fresh Redesign & the ReStyle Group)

A buyer can easily image the wonderful life they will have here.

(Courtesy of Carie Baumann, Fresh Redesign & the ReStyle Group)

Show Storage

Remember that staging is about making buyers believe that this home meets all their needs, including storage. You can address this need very simply by showing extra room in your bedroom furniture. Even though the bookcase in your spare bedroom is going with you, show how much storage is in there by having it only half full of books or treasures—show that there is extra space.

The other logical place people store stuff in bedrooms is under the bed. Maybe you have shoes or holiday wrapping paper under yours, or a box of sweaters or off-season clothes. Storage under the bed is handy and resourceful, but the downside is that it make buyers think that there is so little storage room in your home that you have no choice but to store things under the bed. This is especially true if you can see the items under the bed without lifting a bed skirt or comforter. Your storage items poking out from beneath the bed ruins the allusion of spaciousness and organization.

Another no-no is back-of-the-door hangers. Again, hanging clothes on the back of the door gives the unintentional message that there is not enough storage room in this bedroom, so you've devised other methods to get around that shortcoming.

Arrange the Bedrooms

There are a couple tricks-of-the-staging-trade when arranging furniture to its best advantage. The best part about furniture arranging is that it doesn't cost a thing and usually takes so little time. You may be thinking that if it doesn't cost anything and it's not hard to do, it can't really make all that much difference. The good news is that, indeed, the artful arrangement of furniture, no matter what the room, can highlight its advantages for buyers.

Staging Snafu

Don't forget to make all the beds every day. The single most important staging trick you can do in the bedroom is to make the beds. This includes master beds, children's beds, and even the baby's crib.

The first piece of furniture to place and orient in any bedroom is the focal point, the bed.

The key point for bed placement is that ideally it needs to be across from the door to the room. When you are glancing into the room, the bed should be directly opposite you. Looking at the soothing and calming appearance of a neatly made bed is so much better than having the first glance into the room be a desk or dresser with items on them.

You may have seen beds on an angle out from a corner. This can be done, but it usually requires a large room for the placement to work. The bed angled this way actually takes up more room than it does when oriented any other way.

This is the typical layout of furniture in a master bedroom.

(Software courtesy of Icovia, design courtesy of Julie Dana, The Home Stylist)

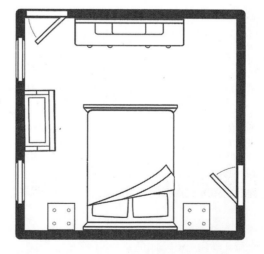

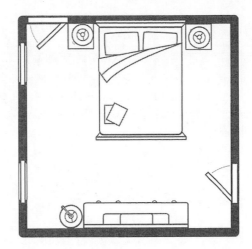

This is what a staged master bedroom looks like, which emphasizes the bedroom's focal point and spaciousness.

(Software courtesy of Icovia, design courtesy of Julie Dana, The Home Stylist)

Any furniture piece that potentially gets cluttered, such as a desk or dresser, and not as tidy as you would like, should go on the same wall as the door. This way, you won't notice or see it as readily when you first glance into the room. Remember, those first impressions are very important.

This alcove adjacent to a child's bedroom has busy wallpaper and lots of clutter.

(Courtesy of Kim Ausbury and Teresa Kratzer, Staged For You)

With the wallpaper removed and playful touches added, it looks like the toys will put themselves away.

(Courtesy of Kim Ausbury and Teresa Kratzer, Staged For You)

Make It Stylish

You may have already realized that you have removed just about anything that makes your room have any personality, and you are probably thinking to yourself, "Who would buy such a boring home?" Well, here is your next step.

This step is so important that, without this step, you really have only cleaned and decluttered your bedrooms. You cannot say you have truly staged your home to sell until you have added specific elements that give it style. And most importantly, it is an impression that makes people want to buy your home.

The staging/decorating message you want in your master bedroom is of a fancy, luxurious hotel spa. Right now, close your eyes and imagine a fancy hotel—look at how the bed is made up, what the bedcovers look like. See what is on the walls, imagine the accessories that are in the room. Now open your eyes and look around your bedroom. What do you need to do to make this room look like the spa you just envisioned?

The staging message you want for your secondary bedrooms are an organized, flexible room that can welcome a child of any age. Look around one of your secondary bedrooms—can a buyer easily imagine one of their children living there? Can a buyer easily convert this bedroom to an office? The easier you make it for that room to meet the buyer's differing needs, the easier it will be for that buyer to purchase your home.

Here are some steps to achieve that look for less.

Make the Bed

The key to achieving the look of a luxurious room is the making of the bed. Even though you may not normally make it this way, or you may need to purchase extra linens or pillows, it will make the difference.

The bedcovers ideally need to be a solid color. This is a very on-trend look. If your current covers are patterned, have you tried flipping the comforter over? There may be a more subdued color or pattern on the other side—and it didn't cost you anything.

If you need to purchase a new bed covering, choose one that looks fancy and expensive, but isn't. Do not purchase or use a country quilt, an animal-themed, or other strongly designated motif. Do purchase one that is expensive looking, and fancy.

Experts Explain

"I like bed-in-a bag—those all-in-one sheets, comforter, shams and bed skirts sets, which usually sell for less than $100. Believe me, setting the stage in the bedrooms really pays off."

—Barb Schwarz, founder of the Home Staging concept and President and CEO of StagedHomes.com

Add a new fresh looking bed skirt that goes all the way to the floor. It gives the bed a feeling of luxury and also finishes the look. Another important element in fancy bed making is pillows. Place the sleeping pillows first with quality pillow cases. Now add at least two large pillows with decorative pillow shams. These are the pillows that are for show and you usually don't rest your head on them at night. Use fluffy pillows and not pillows that have been flattened down from years of use. Last add 2-3 accent pillows to give the bed a feeling of luxury.

This pink patterned bedspread is attractive, but not what you would expect to see at a high-end spa.

(Courtesy of Amy Ross and Beth Sammarone, The Redesign Team)

Spending a few dollars on a luxurious red bedspread and several pillow accessories creates a new, relaxed ambiance in this room.

(Courtesy of Amy Ross and Beth Sammarone, The Redesign Team)

Another option is to get a bedspread, which is a bedcovering that goes to the floor. If you use a bedspread, you won't need a bed skirt. However, you will still need to dress up the bed with pillows.

Now, on to the beds in the secondary bedrooms. These beds should also steer clear of a strong-themed fabric, such as cartoon characters, super heroes, or movie motifs. If you do have one of these types of bedcovers, you can usually flip it over to the other side. It is ok if the other side is plain—you want plain. You can have themed pillows because those are not as dominant. Again, you want the bed skirt to go to the floor.

Room Accessories

Accessories, as with clothing, can make or break the style you aspire to. Finishing touches make a style statement that is memorable. When a person has viewed several homes in one day, you want yours to be remembered for all the right reasons. Style statements and accessories can do that.

In the master bedroom, some things buyers don't want to see are collections, whether your collection includes an impressive array of dolls or a huge collection of baseball cards. The master bedroom is not the place to display them. In staging a master bedroom, you want to clearly see that a grown-up lives there. Your aim should be one of sophisticated hotel.

To add those finishing touches and sellable style, consider one or more of these accessory tips:

◆ Place a novel or magazine on the bedside table.

◆ Toss a throw casually over the end of the bed.

◆ Add a vase of fresh flowers such as romantic roses on the dresser.

◆ Place your knitting project beside your sitting chair.

◆ Hang art that is romantic but not risqué. Artwork featuring couples dancing or sitting together enforces the concept of the dream of the perfect relationship.

◆ Remove picture of family members.

For the secondary bedrooms, we want them as clean and tidy as possible. You want toys to a minimum, but you can have a few.

Remove almost all stuffed animals because so many buyers perceive them as clutter.

To add finishing touches to the secondary rooms, try these tips:

◆ Place one doll or stuffed animal on the bed.

◆ If room, set up a board game or puzzle in progress.

◆ Replace posters with framed art.

◆ Remove personalized name accents.

If You Don't Have Very Many Bedrooms

Some homes, condos, or townhomes only have one or two bedrooms. It can be a little confusing to know what to do, so we'll help.

If you don't clearly have a master bedroom, pick the room with the biggest closets or best view to stage as your master bedroom.

If your place only has one other bedroom and your neighborhood generally attracts other families, try to place two twin beds or a bunk bed in that bedroom.

If you have a guest bedroom—typically the fourth bedroom—set it up much like a master bedroom, with a sophisticated feel. Don't turn it into another child's or grand-child's room. Make it elegant for grownup guests.

If a spare bedroom has morphed into a hobby room, be sure to change it back to a bedroom to get buyers excited about how many bedrooms there are. Remember, their needs are probably different from your needs.

> **Staging Snafu** _____
>
> Make sure bedrooms are obviously bedrooms to any potential buyers. In my neighborhood lived a little old lady in a small two-bedroom ranch. She occupied one bedroom, but because of her frailty, her family moved the washer and dryer up from the basement to the second bedroom, so she didn't have to go down the flight of stairs. Yes, that was thoughtful of them, but now she has moved into an assisted living center and the home is on the market. With the washer and dryer in one bedroom, it looks like it is a one-bedroom home. The simple cure for this home is to move the laundry appliances back to the basement and make up that secondary bedroom as a real bedroom again.

The Least You Need to Know

- Decorate the master bedroom to look and feel like a room in an upscale hotel. Help buyers look forward to coming home to such a relaxing space.

- Depersonalize bedrooms so buyers feel comfortable going in them, and imagining their possessions in them.

- Make any bedroom feel more spacious by removing excess furniture and toys. Get the children involved by having them help you sort their toys and donating some to charity. We all know that toys seem to multiply and can quickly take over a room.

- Adding style to master bedrooms is as easy as taking down family photos, adding a small vase of fresh roses, hanging romantic artwork, placing a soft throw across the end of the bed—small touches to stage the home as a sanctuary for weary owners.

- Stage secondary bedrooms with touches like a board game in progress, placing one doll or toy on the bed, taking down posters and hanging framed artwork. Remember to removing any personalized pieces that prevent buyers from imagining their own children living there.

Chapter 13

The Bathrooms

In This Chapter

- ◆ Making it sparkling clean
- ◆ Keeping primping private
- ◆ De-emphasizing the past
- ◆ Adding a spa-like style

We all know what bathrooms are used for, but besides basic hygiene, they are also used for primping, hair styling, make-up application, bathing, and even getting dressed. They are such private spaces that homeowners often neglect to stage them. Fortunately, you don't have to spend a ton of money to get them looking their best.

The key to staging a bathroom is to suggest all the primping and hygiene happens magically—there should be no evidence of it anywhere in the bathroom, except tucked neatly away in drawers.

We'll show you some simple tricks to make this room a selling feature rather than just a bathroom, starting with simple repairs, decluttering and a thorough cleaning.

Minor Repairs

There are a couple of elements in this room that need to be in top shape and working condition to ensure buyers won't mentally deduct money from your asking price.

Walls

The first noticeable minor repair you can do is to remove wallpaper. Wallpaper is so style and taste-specific that the majority of buyers will not appreciate the beautiful wallpaper you chose.

It can also be overpowering in a small room, as most bathrooms are. Yes, you may love the pattern but many potential buyers will add it to their mental list of projects to be completed as soon as they move in, which reduces the amount they will be willing to pay for your home and might also reduce the likelihood that they'll even make an offer.

To avoid any roadblocks to getting your full asking price, remove any wallpaper in your bathrooms. The same goes for wallpaper borders running across the top of the room or near the chair rail—take them down. Although removing wallpaper is a messy job, the good news is that it is a small room and will cost you little in time or effort to do it yourself.

Buyers can't help but be distracted by this garish wallpaper and matching red carpeting.

(Courtesy of Jennifer Keener, Amazing Transformations)

Removing the wallpaper and carpeting makes the bathroom seem larger and fresher.

(Courtesy of Jennifer Keener, Amazing Transformations)

Just as wallpaper is taste-specific, so are paint treatments, such as sponge painting, ragging, faux finishes, or anything that uses more than one color. You absolutely want the paint in your bathroom to be a solid soft neutral for that fresh look.

Floors

Floors of the bathrooms should also be up-to-date and clean. Up-to-date means that the floor is sturdy—no soft spots underneath where water damage has occurred—from the current decade, and in great shape. If any of those conditions apply—damaged, outdated, or worn—spend the money to shore up the floorboards and recover them with new linoleum or tile. You also do not want carpeting in your bathroom. It is best to pull it up and replace with vinyl sheets or tiles.

Counter

More important than the floor, however, is the bathroom counter. The primary rule is that counters should not be a color. Did I hear you say you have a pink or forest green counter? If at all possible, you should replace it. White or neutral counters are the most valuable to buyers. If replacing the countertop, remember to stay in keeping with other houses in your price range. If your comparables have granite or Corian countertops then you should consider doing the same.

An economical solution for the colored or boldly tiled counter is that it can be painted. There are special primers and paint that will adhere to these slick surfaces. It is a not a permanent solution but it should last a year. Check with your local paint store or home improvement store for the proper product available in your area of the country.

Grout and Caulking

The last minor repair you can probably tackle yourself in the bathroom is replacing *grout* and *caulking*.

Grout around tiles can get easily stained. Even though you have cleaned it many times, it still can get discolored. Stained grout looks dirty and moldy. Applying a new coating of grout can freshen up the whole look of the bathroom with minimal expense. Follow the directions on the tube or container of grout for best results. Your local home improvement store can give you great tips, too.

def•i•ni•tion

Grout is a rigid type of mortar that goes in between tiles and seals them in place. **Caulking** is a slightly flexible vinyl or silicone-based substance used around fixtures, such as bathtubs, to prevent water from seeping underneath.

If the caulking material directly around your bathtub is stained and dirty or chipping away, new caulking will make it look fresh again. It's a fairly easy and inexpensive job for the do-it-yourselfer, with big returns for the effort.

Fan

One fixture that often needs fixing that you may not even notice any more is the bathroom fan. It is a real turn-off to buyers when they flip the light switch in the bathroom, but instead of light, they get the sound of a helicopter taking off. Yeah, you want the fan to make a little noise, but extra loud and strange sounds are a no-no.

As you finish this last detail of the bathroom, you should also remove decorating elements that go with a theme. When selling a home, you don't want a specific theme in your bathroom, such as tropical fish, SpongeBob Squarepants, glamour girl, or a strong nautical theme. Yes, it does add personality, but when you're selling your home, you want the personality to be as low-key and unobtrusive as possible.

Money Maker

There are two no-cost bathroom style tricks that many sellers forget to do. First, always draw the shower curtain closed to create a solid silhouette (it helps prevent mold growth, too). Second, close the lid of the toilet. It is just more polite.

Clean and Declutter

You don't want buyers to see all your primping and hygiene products—you want them to think all that just happens without any work or accessories. So put away all the bottles of shampoo, conditioner, and body wash from the shower ledge. Clear the counter of shaving cream, hairspray, and deodorant.

We also don't want knickknacks in the room. Bathrooms are small to begin with, so adding lots of knickknacks and mementos makes them seem smaller than they are.

This homeowner apparently needed extra space to hold all their toiletries, which are plentiful on this over-the-toilet shelf.

(Courtesy of Carole Julius, Creative Interiors by Carole)

The shelf is removed, stockpile is stored away, walls are painted a soothing blue-green, and upscale accessories finish the look.

(Courtesy of Carole Julius, Creative Interiors by Carole)

Personal Equipment

Other types of products you'll want to clear out while you're decluttering the bathroom are toileting equipment, such as a toddler's potty training chair or an elderly person's elevated toileting chair. Nothing spoils a sale like medical equipment in evidence. Yes, that sounds harsh, but it is the stamp of death on any sale.

If you must have toilet equipment, try to store it in a discreet closet, or fold it and tuck away so it is not so obvious.

Other areas you may want to check for extra clutter include the top of the toilet tank. Also remove any overflowing stacks of magazines or other reading material.

If you have young children, you may have a stack of bathtub toys in the bathroom or tub, and they need to be removed. Keep in mind the spa-like image you are trying to present to buyers. That means presenting a bathroom that is fresh, clean, with few accessories except some well-placed luxury items we'll talk about later.

A Thorough Cleaning

As you know, the bathroom has to be sparking clean before buyers come by. To show you what we mean by sparking clean, get a cotton swab from your bathroom supplies. Can you wipe down the entire bathroom and not get the swab even a little dirty? That is how clean it needs to be. Buyers can be forever turned off if this room is dirty or even appears dirty. Other people's personal dirt—yuck!

You wouldn't think we would need to mention this, but be sure not to leave your dirty clothes on the floor of the bathroom. Don't leave clothes or wet towels in the bathroom because a buyer could request a showing at a moment's notice, and you don't want to have to go around picking up clothing off the floor.

Also be sure to have the toilet plunger and toilet bowl scrubbers completely out of sight. No strangers want to see these.

Staging to Sell

The great news is of all the rooms in your home, bathrooms are one of the least expensive to stage. With just a few purchases, you can get a handsome return on your money.

Experts Explain

"If you're wondering where to put your money to help you get top dollar from your home, a bathroom is a good investment. People may or may not make an offer based on the condition of these much-used spaces. A new countertop can dramatically update the bath, making the cabinetry or other elements seem newer by association. A decorative mirror, rather than a medicine chest or frameless mirror, is another way to give a hardworking space visual interest. The best thing of all, though, is elbow grease. Every surface should sparkle!"

—*Designed to Sell: Smart Ideas that pay off!*

Enlarging the Bathroom

Of course, you can't rearrange the bathroom to make it appear spacious, but there are a few things you can do to make the room feel more spacious:

- Make sure you have good lighting. Bright light is necessary in bathrooms.
- Remove extra shelving or plastic drawers. It may make it more convenient for you to use, but it will make buyers think the bathroom is just too tiny.

◆ Make sure mirror is not cracked or aged. Consider replacing a full counter length mirror with a slightly smaller framed mirror, which is more current.

◆ Remove the several small scatter rugs, such as the contoured rug, bath mat, etc., and exchange them for one larger rug. It unifies the appearance and makes the room appear spacious.

The Spa Image

The key word to shoot for in preparing your bathrooms is, "spa-like." You want buyers to peek into any of your bathrooms and have the impression that they are luxurious places to rest. The good news is that this spa-like atmosphere is easy to achieve, even for less creative people.

This bathroom shows cleaning products out and small scatter rugs.

(Courtesy of Kim Ausbury and Teresa Kratzer, Staged For You)

With clutter away and nice spa-like touches, the bathroom and house are ready to buy.

(Courtesy of Kim Ausbury and Teresa Kratzer, Staged For You)

Let's tackle the most seemingly difficult obstacle in decorating a bathroom: a colored bathroom counter or fixtures. We understand that you can't always replace them, although that is our first recommendation. If you need to compromise on budget, here is what you should and shouldn't do to downplay those permanent colors.

Do not accessorize the bathrooms with the same color you are trying to de-emphasize. For example, if your toilet and counters are pink, do not place pink rugs or a pink shower curtain in that space—it only emphasizes the color choice. Instead, with a little searching, you can find a mixture of a neutral color with the pink. For example, a beige or brown shower curtain with some pink in it would be good, then add all beige towels to play up the complementary color instead of the dominant pink.

If your bathroom fixtures are blue, try adding a neutral color, such as soft grays, for a seascape palette. Just add a shimmery silver shower curtain—very spa-like—and a few thick gray or silver shades of towels for a much preferred glamorous look. You just changed from the 1960s to a present day chic.

What if your fixtures are white and you no longer have wallpaper to jazz up the room—it's now seemingly boring and uninspiring. Easy. Pick one light neutral color (such as beige, taupe or light sage green) and add contrast with the addition of the shower curtain and towels. Add some live greens to the space and voila, a great room. Keep the color palette to a sophisticated combination of one neutral and one color. You can't go wrong. Keeping it simple makes the bathroom feel larger and cleaner.

The two most important purchases you will need for each bathroom are: a new glamorous shower curtain and thick fluffy towels. These declare spa and "ah!" to buyers. Replace the liner behind your shower curtain to make sure there is no possibility of mold or mildew on the liner.

When purchasing towels, look for thick towels to fold, or roll them to appear even thicker. Thick towels even look thicker when folded as small as possible, with seams folding inside. Remember you can never go wrong with thick white or cream towels.

Both nice towels and expensive-looking bath accessories can be found at major bath and linen retailers. And the bonus is you can take them with you to your new home.

Additional bathroom accessories to pick up while you are shopping are:

◆ One or two small thick candles

◆ Pretty guest soaps

◆ A decorative liquid soap dispenser

Now imagine your staged master bathroom: no cosmetics or hygiene products in sight, and sparkling clean. Glamorous shower curtain, thick towels nicely folded on the towel rack. On the counter is nothing but a candle and pretty dish of guest soaps. You've achieved a spa-like look and feel for less than $50.

Experts Explain

"Open a bathroom window if your bathroom has one, and place a small bouquet of fresh flowers or an aloe plant on the sill or vanity. Choose an innovative vase such as a little pitcher, antique bottle, or interesting candy tin. The fresh cheerful image of flowers combined with the pleasant surprise of the curious little vase will position the bathroom in the buyer's mind as a fresh, beautiful space."

—Martha Webb, author of *Dress Your House for Success; 5 Fast, Easy Steps to Selling Your House, Apartment or Condo for the Highest Possible Price*

Other than bathing products and a random towel, this bathroom has little pizzazz.

(Courtesy of Carole Julius, Creative Interiors by Carole)

But with a new shower curtain, fluffy towels, a coordinating rug, and greenery, the room is much more special.

(Courtesy of Carole Julius, Creative Interiors by Carole)

The Powder Room

What about the small half-bath or the other full bath? The spa-like look needs to be consistent throughout the home. Think how disappointed a buyer would be if one bathroom is tranquil and glamorous but the other bathrooms have blow dryers, curling irons, electric razors, and stacks of inappropriate reading material for families. You just ruined the magical illusion of behind-the-scenes hygiene and primping.

Staging Snafu

One staging trick used years ago was to fill the bathtub with water and add floating candles or flower petals. Don't do it. Sometimes couples will tour properties with small children and a tub full of water and lit candles, with distracted parents focusing elsewhere, is just asking for trouble.

Now a note for vacant homes. We'll discuss this a little more in Chapter 17, but a quick note here will help remind you. If your home is vacant but the water is still on, please leave a roll of toilet paper in the bathroom. If your home has the water turned off, a small note taped to the bathroom door would be kindly appreciated. Enough said.

The Least You Need to Know

- ◆ Make the bathroom the cleanest room in your home.

- ◆ Remove all hygiene and primping products from view.

- ◆ Take down wallpaper and any accessories related to a theme, such as nautical or SpongeBob Squarepants.

- ◆ De-emphasize the built-in, dated color palette on your counters or toilet by introducing accessories like a shower curtain and towels that have a complementary color. Then play up that second color to balance the existing color.

- ◆ Add a few spa-like accessories such as candles, guest soaps, or a liquid soap dispenser.

Chapter 14

The Closets

In This Chapter

- ◆ Staging a closet to look more spacious
- ◆ Minor repairs that add value
- ◆ Style tips that wow buyers
- ◆ Creating space where there isn't any

Home buyers like storage space—lots of it. No matter how large the rooms are in a home, if there aren't closets and places in which to put things away, it will be a harder sell. Making the most of the closet space you have is key to getting the most dollar for your home.

Fortunately, with a little guidance, you can show buyers your home has all the storage space they'll need. From linen closets to pantries to hall closets and mudrooms, any and all of these areas are prime real estate for home-buyers. Staging your closets effectively comes down to showing off all your existing space to full advantage and removing any visual suggestions that the closets are inadequate. We'll show you how.

Show There Is Room to Grow

If you remember nothing else with respect to closets, remember that they all need to be only half full. Buyers want to be reassured that there is plenty of space in the closets to hold all their belongings—seeing half-empty closets is reassuring to them. Of course, that means that you're going to have to remove half of what's currently in each of your closets.

Match Closet and Purpose

To decide what should stay and what should go, think about the closet's purpose. Is it a linen closet? Is it a kitchen pantry? Is it a clothing closet? Each closet has its own unique purpose and it is important to match appropriate possessions to the particular closet, so as not to confuse buyers.

For instance, you wouldn't put snow boots in the kitchen pantry, next to the boxes of noodles or soup. Nor would you have out-of-season clothes in the linen closet—only blankets, towels, and bedding belong there. When buyers open closet doors and find unexpected items, their first assumption is that there wasn't enough space elsewhere to store things where they belong. Even if that's true, you don't want to confirm it. Instead, be sure that each closet is stocked appropriately:

- Coat—coats, umbrellas, hats, gloves
- Linen—pillows, bedding, towels
- Hall—games, toys, sports equipment
- Bedroom—clothing, shoes
- Pantry—food, canned goods
- Mudroom—out-of-season outer wear, shoes, boots
- Laundry—laundry detergent, ironing board, iron

Money Maker _____

When your home is being shown, be sure to close all the doors—including closets—to present a neater appearance throughout.

No matter what the closet's purpose, all should be only half-full, not stuffed to the gills or ready to erupt when opened. In addition to seeing shelf and hanging spaces within closets, buyers also need to be able to see the floor.

Money Maker _____

According to the National Association of Realtors, "Homebuyers are willing to pay more for the features they desire. Among buyers who purchased a home without a desired feature, 66 percent would pay extra for a walk-in closet in their master bedroom (a median of $825 more)." Keep this in mind as you consider repairs and additions.

Most closets look like this one—stuffed and unkempt.

(Courtesy of Eric Straith, photographer)

Even just clearing the closet out makes an amazing improvement.

(Courtesy of Eric Straith, photographer)

Minor Repairs Worth Doing

In addition to being only partially full, closets also need to function properly. That is, the door needs to open easily and close securely. The shelves need to be sturdy and straight. Any hanging rods need to be up, and there should be a working ceiling light.

Most of these repairs or upgrades can be done with a screwdriver and screws or nails. If you don't already have a ceiling light, you may need to install one or hire a handyman to put it in. But start first by checking to see if you merely have a burned out light bulb—then replace it with the maximum wattage allowed, to make the closet as bright as possible.

If the door does not open or close easily, the problem may be the carpeting. Frequently doors work fine until new carpeting is installed, and then there isn't enough clearance for the door to swing open easily. The solution is to take the door off the hinges and shave the bottom of the door down. Yes, it's a little unwieldy, but not hard to do.

Also if the doorknob isn't working, or it isn't latching, consider investing in a new knob. If the knob is fine, perhaps it's the size of the opening for the latch—you may need to enlarge the catch space on the door trim.

In addition to being a total mess organizationally, this closet is dark and uninviting.

(Courtesy of Amy Ross and Beth Sammarone, The Redesign Team)

Simply fixing the light bulb and straightening the shelves dramatically improves this pantry's appearance.

(Courtesy of Amy Ross and Beth Sammarone, The Redesign Team)

Play Up All the Space

Many homes have all—or nearly all—the closet space the inhabitants need, but through the years, that storage capacity becomes overloaded with clutter. So your first step in showing off your ample closet space is to declutter, clean, and brighten it.

Declutter

For simplicity's sake, you might want to completely empty each closet as you work, clearing out everything that has been tucked away there, so you can more easily assess what should be there, and what should be stored elsewhere, given away, or thrown away.

Money Maker

Aim to keep about 20 percent of your wardrobe—the 20 percent you wear frequently. Then pack away the other 80 percent to be moved to your new home.

Store off-season clothes in another part of the house, such as a storage tub in the basement or garage. Pack away extras, such as toiletries and clothes the kids will eventually grow into, that you want to move, but which you won't need in the next couple of months. You don't need to keep things like that in the closets. Throw away ripped and ratty towels and sheets, donate coats and mittens that no longer fit or suit your tastes, and donate or discard food items from your pantry that you know you'll never eat (that's the stuff to donate), as well as the cans that have long since expired (that's the stuff to discard).

Money Maker _____

If you have open bags or containers of pet food, use a chip clip to seal off the tops. Or, if it will fit, put the bag into a zip lock bag and seal the top. Pet food has an odor that can be offensive to some, so this will get rid of the scent.

As you begin to put things back into closets, remember the rule—only half full. That applies to shelves—meaning that only half the shelves are full, hanging rods—leave plenty of space and a few extra hangers, and floor space. Of course, that doesn't mean you can't use the floor, just that there should only be a couple of pairs of shoes, or appliances, or toys, depending on the closet's purpose, rather than 100.

Clean

As with any kind of cleaning, start at the top and move down. Dust the light fixture and around the ceiling, to get rid of cobwebs. Then dust upper shelves and move down. Wipe off any hanging rods. Then vacuum or sweep the floor of the closet.

Make sure there are no clothes on the floor of a linen or bedroom closet, nor any food on the floor in the pantry. Not only does it look messy, but it prevents buyers from being able to see the floor.

Brighten

As previously recommended, make sure there is a light fixture in the closet—either on the door or on the ceiling—that it has the maximum wattage allowed in the socket, and that the glass or plastic cover is clean and free of dust and bugs. Going through those steps nearly guarantees your closet will immediately appear brighter and more spacious.

Wiping down any mirror on the interior door is also a good idea, for cleanliness and light reflection.

Staging Your Closet to Sell

After decluttering, cleaning, and brightening your closet, the final step is to make some small changes that will significantly affect how buyers view your closets and your home.

Essentially, when buyers open your closets and peer into them, you want them to believe you're obsessive-compulsive—that you're super tidy. Because if you're this careful about how you keep your closets, you probably are equally meticulous in how you take care of the property. Just like that, the perceived value of your home increased.

To give an aura of perfectionism within your closets, it all comes down to systematic organization. That is, like items go with like items, like sizes go with like sizes, and they are all lined up perfectly on the shelves and on hangers.

 Staging Snafu _____

> Don't invest in expensive closet organizing systems, or custom shelving, in the hopes of impressing buyers. It may look nice, but it's unlikely the configuration you choose will exactly match their own needs. If you already have one, don't take it out, but don't spend money on a new organizing system and expect to get your investment back.

The Kitchen Pantry

Potential buyers have the right and will look behind all kinds of closed doors. Nothing is off-limits when selling a home. Buyers should see the epitome of organization in pantries, cabinets and closets. Arrange like items with like such as boxes of noodles grouped together, spaghetti sauces together, canned vegetables together, etc. All products should be lined up in rows facing forward, with the product labels facing out so you can easily see what they are.

Your pantry shelves should match a grocery store's shelves. Don't go so far as to put brand names together, but face the shelves with the tallest items on the end and work in so the shortest items are in the middle.

Make sure you're leaving half the shelves clear—no food or pantry items on them at all—to show off how much extra space you have available for the new owner to enjoy.

Experts Explain _____

"The fact that you don't have enough closet space may even be the primary reason you want to sell your home. If that's the case, you've got a tough challenge ahead. What you need to do is meet your prospective buyer's expectations that you have more than enough closet space for everything you own."

—Ilyce Glink in *50 Simple Steps You Can Take to Sell Your Home Faster and for More Money In Any Market*

The Linen Closet

What's key in the linen closet is the quality of the folding.

When folding flat sheets, the best strategy is to fold them in half length-wise, then fold them in half width-wise. Then fold them again in half length-wise and in half width-wise. Finally, fold them in thirds and place them on the shelf.

When folding fitted sheets, fold them in half length-wise and then in half width-wise. Tuck the corners inside each other and smooth. Then fold them in half or in thirds.

In order to have neat piles of similar sizes within the closet, follow some or all of these tips for tidy piles in your linen closet:

♦ When placing sheets inside the linen closet, put the fitted sheet on the bottom because it tends to be bulkier. The flat sheet folded on top looks nicer.

♦ Another trick to achieve uniformity of folding is to place the flat and fitted sheets, folded, into their matching pillow case so that everything is together.

♦ Some sellers have been known to take sheet sets to the dry cleaners to be washed, folded, and pressed or starched. They use those sets for "show" inside the closet, washing and replacing the same ones on the bed each week.

♦ If you have more sheets but can't or don't want to pack them up yet, try putting several layers on your bed at once—fitted, flat, then fitted, flat, and top with a fitted to hold it all down. Changing sheets to wash is easy—just strip off the top layer and you are all set with fresh ones. It is a real time saver for busy people.

After you've removed at least half of what was previously there, fold the remaining items crisply and neatly. Then place like items together—bath towels on top of bath towels, hand towels stacked neatly, and wash cloths stacked similarly. Neatness counts for a lot here.

It's hard to see into this linen closet, with bedding falling off the shelves and jammed into the space.

(Courtesy of Amy Ross and Beth Sammarone, The Redesign Team)

By removing some of the contents and spending time folding, this linen closet is now neat as a pin.

(Courtesy of Amy Ross and Beth Sammarone, The Redesign Team)

The Master Bedroom Closet

In your master bedroom closet, which likely consists mainly of hanging space, group like clothing together—pants with pants, blouses with blouses, suits with suits, etc. If you want to color group them within each type of apparel, that can further confirm your obsessive nature (which is what you want to imply).

On the floor, line up your recently-shined shoes facing forward. But remember that no more than 50 percent of the closet floor should be covered with anything, so don't put out too many pairs of shoes.

A mishmash of hangers looks busy and unkempt.

(Courtesy of Amy Ross and Beth Sammarone, The Redesign Team)

Replacing unmatched wire and plastic hangers with uniform wooden ones transforms the closet into an upscale space.

(Courtesy of Amy Ross and Beth Sammarone, The Redesign Team)

Staging Snafu _____

Remove all wire hangers from your closets and replace them with molded plastic or wooden hangers. Wire hangers are a big no-no in staging because they're cheap looking, get easily tangled, and don't allow clothes to hang properly—especially suits and wool pieces.

The Coat Closet

Depending on what you typically store here, follow the same guidelines as you did with previous closets to clear them out, clean them up, and put back a fraction of the contents grouped together by purpose. Hats, mittens, and gloves might be placed in a plastic storage box on a top shelf, while coats are grouped together on hangers. Boots could be cleaned and lined up neatly on the floor.

The Hall Closet

Those miscellaneous closets, where you may be storing everything from toys to throws to sports equipment, can be staged by following the same rules we just mentioned.

The owners make the most of this closet, storing shoes on the door and filling it with everything from coats to a vacuum, to miscellaneous junk, making it seem tiny.

(Courtesy of Amy Ross and Beth Sammarone, The Redesign Team)

Staging your closets—neatening them up—costs you absolutely nothing and makes a huge positive impression on potential buyers. The message you send is that if you've taken such good care of your closets, you've probably taken equally good care of the home itself. You're adding dollars to your bottom line every time you turn a can of peas face-forward in your kitchen pantry.

Stripping it down to only a few hanging items and a small box on the shelf and on the floor, buyers can see how much space is actually available—certainly a lot more than was visible before.

(Courtesy of Amy Ross and Beth Sammarone, The Redesign Team)

Creating the Illusion of Space

If you live in a home that is lacking storage space—maybe you don't have a linen closet, or the bedroom closets you have are way too small—we have some tips for helping buyers to overlook it.

Most people won't notice if a particular type of closet is missing in your home, such as a linen closet or coat closet, if you don't make it obvious that you're having trouble finding places to put what normally go in such a closet.

Don't try and compensate for the fact that you don't have a hall closet by setting up a hall tree for coats. Not only does it look messy, with all the coats draped over it, but it makes it blatantly clear to buyers that you're lacking space to hang guests' coats.

Similarly, don't stack food on the counters—even if you do it neatly with the labels facing forward—because it screams "we don't have enough cabinet space" to anyone who walks through the kitchen. Pack it up and move it elsewhere.

Some sellers put hooks on the back of a door for coats and excess clothing. While this isn't a perfect solution, it's much, much better than putting up a coat tree.

Another idea, for any home with a basement, is to put hooks up going down the basement wall on the side that doesn't have the hand railing. Here you can hang coats, sports gear, and seasonal wear you don't need everyday.

Money Maker

For help and inspiration in determining how to best organize your closet, skim the pages of home decorating and women's magazines for pictures of what an organized closet typically looks like. You may find storage solutions and products you weren't aware of, too.

The Least You Need to Know

- Closets that are neat and only half-full suggest to buyers that there is plenty of space to store their own belongings.

- It's important for buyers to be able to see the floor of the closet, to accurately gauge its total size.

- What is left in closets—after you've removed at least half of the contents— should be neatly folded, placed in tidy rows, with product labels facing forward, if applicable, as someone who is obsessed with tidiness would likely do.

- Don't try and compensate for a lack of space by putting up a coat tree or hanging extra hooks on the walls—it only makes the lack of a closet more apparent to buyers.

Chapter 15

The Home Office

In This Chapter

- ◆ Keeping the focus on work
- ◆ Tidying cords and desks
- ◆ Using feng shui principles
- ◆ Balancing bedrooms and office space

The need for home office space is increasing as employees and self-employed folks alike spend more and more time working from home. Some corporate employees are being asked to set up shop at home, rather than take up space in expensive offices, while others are requesting the opportunity to work from home each week, rather than having to drive to an office building. And once conducting work at home becomes a regular event, the need for a separate office generally emerges.

Setting up a home office isn't difficult, if you don't already have one, and generally involves taking over an existing bedroom. But there are things you'll want to avoid as you stage this room to its best advantage.

Setting Up a Home Office

What dens were in the 1960s and 1970s, home offices are for the 1990s and 2000s. They are a work space for one or more members of the family, where productivity is the theme.

Staging a room as a home office makes sense if you have at least three bedrooms—if you have three or less, don't do it. But with four or more, it's a good idea to convert a spare bedroom into a home office. And, if you have the option, use a room on the first floor, rather than the second, as the office—it's more accessible and professional, especially if you expect client visits.

Experts Explain _____

Not sure that a home office will be of interest to working adults looking at your home? According to technology research company Gartner Inc., more than 23 percent of the U.S. workforce worked at least one day a month at home in 2005. That figure is expected to grow to 27 percent of the workforce by 2008.

Remember Its Purpose

As you're staging a home office, keep in mind its primary purpose, which is to get work done. Although such rooms often become catch-all spaces, into which home-work and other projects are corralled, you need to reclaim it as a work room only.

If you have any of the following items currently in the home office space, remove it:

◆ Exercise equipment

◆ A television

◆ Toys

◆ Out-of-season clothing

◆ Craft projects

◆ Laundry tools, such as an ironing board

◆ Bed

The office needs to be sleek, organized, and neat. You want buyers who enter the room to be struck by how efficient it looks. They should think to themselves: "Wow, I could get so much done here!"

No matter where your office area is, it should be a selling feature.

(Courtesy of Gina McNew, diva la difference interiors)

This bonus office space now looks ready for buyers. This space will make chores seem a breeze.

(Courtesy of Gina McNew, diva la difference interiors)

Creative Spaces

If you're in a creative field, such as graphic design or art, you can certainly show the fruits of your labor around the room, but it's important to feature it as a tidy work space. Just as paper intensive workers wouldn't want to overwhelm buyers with papers everywhere, make sure you don't have an abundance of canvases, sketches, or drawings lying about. The biggest difference between the two types of spaces may be that instead of having a computer as your primary work tool, you may have an easel or a drawing table front and center.

But then around that central tool, show how organized you are, with a few file folders or colored pencils—whatever you use—out with a project in process.

Declutter and Clean

In cleaning up or creating a home office, the focus should be on reducing the amount of papers that are scattered throughout. Getting rid of papers you no longer need, or filing away those you do, will significantly improve the appearance of your office and will suggest to buyers that you are one organized worker.

Computer "Décor"

One of the biggest annoyances in the office is computer cords. Not only do they get tangled and look unsightly, but it's often hard to cover them up. One solution is to position the back of your desk against a wall—never face a desk into the room, with computer wires and cables draping down the front of the desk. Either move the computer to the side, where the cords are less visible, or back the desk up to the wall and hide them altogether.

In addition to hiding computer cords and cables, you should also wipe them off as you're cleaning the office. Computer cords tend to attract a lot of dust and can appear as if they haven't been touched in decades after just a few weeks. Take a dust cloth and run it over the wires to release the dust bunnies.

Money Maker

With so many computer accounts and services we now have to manage, many people end up posting scraps of paper around the computer or desk listing passwords for the services they use most. If that describes you, make sure you take them down before strangers start touring your home or you're effectively allowing them access to your most guarded accounts.

This house had plenty of bedrooms but no home office. This room also had dated light fixtures.

(Courtesy of Linda Pellien, Home Finishing Touches)

This new versatile office greets buyers.

(Courtesy of Linda Pellien, Home Finishing Touches)

Closet Considerations

If you have a closet in your home office, it doesn't have to hold 100 percent work-related products, but it should be neat and half-full, just like all the rest of your closets.

Do what you can to clear out old papers and files, and straighten office supplies you have stored there so that it doesn't look like a jumble.

And if you're in need of office organizing products to get things under control, some of the most common purchases made for staging a home office include:

- File trays
- Paper clip holders
- Desk supplies
- File folders

Lighting Necessities

As with other rooms, lighting in the home office should be as bright as possible, with illumination coming from outside as well as in.

All the lights—overhead, table lamps, and floor lamps—should work properly, and any curtains or window treatments should be removed so as not to block any outside light. Rarely is privacy an issue in a home office, so taking down curtains shouldn't be a major concern.

One light you'll want to make sure you have, in addition to the overhead variety, is a table lamp on your desk. It shouldn't be huge, but it should provide light to your work area.

Furniture Arranging

Since *Feng Shui* seems to be all the rage in organizing corporate office spaces, we recommend taking a look at the principles as you organize your home office.

def•i•ni•tion

Feng Shui is the ancient Chinese art of placement that brings harmony to your shelter and assists in the flow of chi, the life force/spirit.

One of the major principles of Feng Shui as it relates to offices is that you should never sit with your back to the door. Not being able to see who comes into the room is not wise, and leaves you at a disadvantage. However, having the desk facing the door puts you in a power position—just watch out for how the computer cords fall.

You also don't want your computer facing the door, presumably for the same reason—you don't want others to see what you're working on without your knowing it.

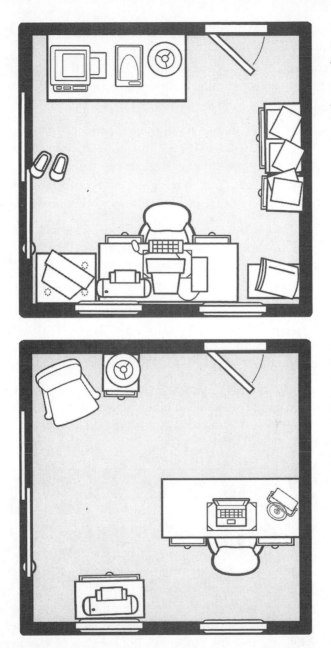

This office shows a room with too much extra furniture and equipment.

(Software courtesy of Icovia, design courtesy of Julie Dana, The Home Stylist)

Reducing the number of work surfaces and adding an upholstered chair makes the room seem bigger and more comfortable for visitors.

(Software courtesy of Icovia, design courtesy of Julie Dana, The Home Stylist)

Although such rearranging may interfere somewhat with your productivity, don't make so many changes that you can't work at all while the home is on the market. That's counterproductive. Instead, rearrange as much as you can, but make sure your computer and files are accessible when you do need to work.

Styling

There are few elements you'll want to add to stage a home office beyond a few organizing tools. The key is to project an image of organization and productivity, so that buyers will perceive the office as a place where work gets done.

Experts Explain

"To help keep your home office organized, color code your files."

—Linda A. Birkinbine, MLS of Keep It Organized, LLC

A simple way to signal productivity is to set up "in" and "out" trays on your desk or credenza. There should be nothing in the "in" box and a large stack in the "out" box, again, subtly communicating that this is a place where serious work gets done.

You can hang a few awards or diplomas on the wall as well—and this is the only room where such professional certificates are permitted. Keep them discreet and nicely framed and hung on a side wall.

If you have a bulletin board to help you manage your work load, or to display family photos and mementos, you have two options: (1) you can take everything down and leave a blank board or (2) you can leave a few items on the board, but they need to be lined up neatly in the center, not hanging haphazardly off the side.

If you have a bookcase in the home office, take as much out as you need to so that it is half full. You can have a mixture of work binders, books, and reference manuals alongside framed photos and nice accessories. But make sure it appears there is plenty of room for expansion.

This office and bookcases do not look professional and ready for buyers.

(Courtesy of Laviza Shariff, Revelations Home Staging and Redesign)

The focal point of the office is this bookcase. Now that it is neat and organized, it will appeal to everyone.

(Courtesy of Laviza Shariff, Revelations Home Staging and Redesign)

Putting away extraneous office equipment that you only use from time-to-time will also make the office appear larger and less cluttered. If you routinely use a laser printer for daily correspondence, unplug the color printer for those times when you're preparing a proposal. Or unplug your fax machine, which you use much less frequently these days, and place it in your half-empty closet until you need to send one.

It's best to remove any filing cabinets you have, perhaps moving them to the basement, to make the room bigger and to suggest that the work gets done by itself in the office. If you have to have access to some critical files everyday, perhaps you can hang them in a drawer in your desk. Or if worse comes to worse, keep one filing cabinet in the room.

Some couples work together, sharing a home office, and have two or more separate desks set up. Although this may work fine for them, when selling your home, you'll need to take one desk out—or as many as you need to so that you're only left with one in the space. Keep the nicest looking desk in the room, taking out the less attractive ones.

This office does not look like you can get a lot of work done.

(Courtesy of Donna Tanfani, Staging NetWorks)

With an organized office, it helps buyers imagine getting lots of work done.

(Courtesy of Donna Tanfani, Staging NetWorks)

The Least You Need to Know

- If you have fewer than four bedrooms, don't set up a home office in one of them. But another spare room, such as a den or playroom, could work just as well.

- The impression you want buyers to have of your office is that it is well-organized and enhances productivity. Make sure it is neat and tidy.

- Feng shui principles can be useful in arranging the office, such as placing the desk so that it faces the door.

- Hide computer cords and cables as much as possible after cleaning off the dust. Nothing looks more unattractive and messy than many computer cords hanging all over the desk.

- The home office is the only room where it is okay to hang diplomas and awards, though you should still keep them somewhat discreet—not hang them over the desk, for example.

Chapter

The Basement, Garage, and Attic

In This Chapter

- ◆ Showing off extra space
- ◆ When to break staging rules
- ◆ Accessibility is key
- ◆ Staging your laundry area

In previous chapters, we've talked about the importance of defining the purpose of each room in your home, whether it was for working, sleeping, or cooking, for example. But in these three spaces—the basement, garage, and attic—that rule does not apply. In fact, these rooms are best kept undefined—additional space that is flexible enough to be used for virtually any purpose.

But even if you only have one or two of these areas, keep the same general objective in mind—showing the space as flexible enough to meet any buyer's potential needs. That means highlighting its cleanliness, brightness, and usability, without a particular purpose.

The Basement

Depending on the condition and size of your basement, it can be used for so many different things.

Unfinished Basement

If you have an unfinished basement, make sure the stairs leading down to it are clean, sturdy, and that there is a handrail for buyers to hold onto. Because most basements are used primarily for storage, there is a tendency not to pay as much attention to the stairway and walls leading to it. Take a look at the stairs with the eyes of a buyer to make sure they look safe and secure.

Basements can make people uncomfortable, even scared, so you'll want to do everything you can to encourage buyers to take the time to go see it. You'll also want to make the doorway and stairs to the basement easily accessible, to make it clear you have nothing to hide from potential buyers.

Once downstairs, you'll want to check for any structural defects, like cracks in the walls or floor. If you find them, have them patched and painted. Minor cracks you can probably take care of yourself with some guidance from your local home improvement store, but if there appears to be significant damage, you may want to call in a professional to advise you on what needs to be done to correct any problems.

> ### Experts Explain
>
> "Color is an important aspect of selling a home. My experience in staging homes all over the country is that blues and greys are the slowest colors to sell interior and exterior. To sell quickly, paint the home in a warm color palette."
>
> —JoAnne Lenart-Weary, "The Queen of Decorating" www.onedaydecorating.com

If you have walls that can be painted, apply bright white paint. While upstairs the recommended wall colors were cream hues, like off-white and beige, downstairs, where it's dark, you want to add as much brightness as possible—get the brightest white you can find.

If you have paneling on the walls, you should seriously consider sanding and painting it white, both to update and brighten the space. Paneling is a very dated look. Because all the mechanical systems are in the basement, the dated paneling makes buyers think that the mechanics are probably dated, too. Painting the paneling is one of the most common suggestions that professional stagers make in a basement.

And on the floor, assuming you have bare concrete, apply grey paint. It will make the floors appear clean, well taken care of, and in excellent shape.

Finished Basement

If you have a finished basement, with a ceiling, floor, and painted walls that feel more like a large room than storage, set it up as extra living space. That means staging it either as a living room, playroom, or guest bedroom, depending on how you're currently using it. Just don't leave it as a blank slate, as you would with an unfinished basement.

Declutter and Clean That Basement

Besides sweeping the floor and straightening the contents of your basement, you may not have thought about doing much cleaning, right? Unless you have a finished basement, you may not even spend much time down there. But because buyers will be inspecting every inch of your home, you'll want to have your basement as sparkling clean as possible.

That starts with using a damp cloth to wipe down your furnace and hot water heater to clean them off. You know buyers will want to check them out, to see what kind of condition they are in, and how old they are. By investing a few minutes in cleaning them off, you may suggest to the buyers that the systems are newer than they are. And newer means higher value.

If you have storage boxes in your basement—and who doesn't—try to consolidate what you have into larger boxes, to reduce the appearance of clutter. Rather than having 10 small boxes stacked against the walls, try and reduce them to 5, or even 3, larger boxes, which looks much neater.

And if you've had those boxes in storage for quite a while, consider going through them and getting rid of anything you won't need or want in your new home. Have a garage sale, call Volunteers of America for a pick up, or throw away anything that is no longer usable. You'll reduce the number of boxes you have to haul up from the basement on moving day, and you'll increase the amount of space buyers will see, and appreciate, when they come to tour.

Money Maker

If storage space becomes scarce in your basement, make more use of available vertical storage areas. Hang bikes and tools on the walls, for example, and use rafters to hold out-of-season equipment, such as sleds or skis.

If you have an area where you collect recyclable bottles before returning them for the deposit, now is the time to clean up that area and get rid of all the bottles and cans that have accumulated.

Likewise, see if you have anything hazardous to be disposed of, such as:

- Paint cans
- Oil
- Solvents and cleaning fluids
- Computers
- Tires
- Scraps of lumber

Investigate where you need to bring these items and clear them out of the basement now, rather than later. The last thing you want buyers to see is piles of potentially hazardous, or annoying, junk laying around in the basement. They may worry that if you leave it, they'll be faced with clearing it out themselves.

Removing Odors from Down Below

Basements can be musty or stuffy, and the best way to reduce any odors is simply to open any windows and doors to the space for a day. Then do it again right before any buyers are scheduled to come through.

Depending on which part of the country you live in, consider adding a humidifier or dehumidifier. The humidifier will add moisture, reducing stuffiness, while the de-humidifier will remove any wetness, getting rid of potential sources of musty smells.

If the basement is where you keep your cat's litter box, make time everyday to clean it out. Since the air does not circulate as well in the basement, litter box odors can quickly build up and impact a buyer's interest in your home.

Make It Bright and Spacious

Since many people don't like spending time in the basement, you need to make it inviting so they'll take the time to explore how much extra space is down there. To do that, you need to make it as bright as possible. That means putting high wattage light bulbs in any light sockets available as well as adding floor lamps.

Another important step is removing any curtains or window treatments from windows. You may lose a little privacy, but how much did you really need in the basement anyway, and you'll gain a lot in extra light from outdoors.

Once you've removed the curtains, wash the windows inside and out to brighten them up and reinforce how clean the space is. You want buyers to say, "Even the basement was light and bright—love this house!"

The lighter and brighter the area is, the larger it will feel and the more willing buyers may be to consider it valuable real estate.

Money Maker

It's a good idea to give your real estate agent a tour of your home before they bring any potential buyers through. During that tour, point out where all the light switches are so that they don't fumble around trying to find them.

Establishing Living Zones

Unlike other areas in your home, basements—and especially large ones—have multiple use zones. That is, you probably use your basement for more than one activity, and you'll want to clearly delineate where each of those activities occurs. For instance, you may have a play area for your children in one corner, a hobby area in another, and a workshop in another. It's important to separate those living areas so buyers can see how useable and flexible the space is.

The quickest and easiest way to accomplish this is with inexpensive bound carpet remnants. Buying a large rug to anchor each area makes it clear to buyers where the hobby area begins and ends, for instance. You should be able to find a plain bound 5 by 8-foot Berber remnant for around $30 in most markets.

Although fairly neat, this basement has undefined zones of packed boxes, games, and living space.

(Courtesy of Amy Ross and Beth Sammarone, The Redesign Team)

By clearing out the boxes and creating a living room feel, this basement looks roomier and more usable.

(Courtesy of Amy Ross and Beth Sammarone, The Redesign Team)

Adding Style to Your Basement

If your basement has a bar area, make sure you don't have a lot of liquor out. One or two bottles of wine are okay. On the other hand, the college fraternity house look is not the upscale image you're going for. Take down any posters or homage to drinking that might offend some buyers. A bar is great as long as it is sophisticated looking.

If you have a play area, tidying it up is all that is really needed. It's best if the toys and games can be confined to one zone, however, rather than spreading across the entire room. This is also the place to encourage the children with your help of course, to eliminate broken toys or toys they have outgrown. You may donate the better toys or sell them at your garage sale.

Another styling trick is to set up a game or puzzle in progress to remind buyers that this is a great recreation area to spend time with friends and family.

Staging Snafu

Don't forget to pick up and remove any critter traps you may have set in the basement before buyers come through. The last thing you want them to see, in addition to all the extra space, is a dead mouse, squirrel, or rat.

If you have a hobby bench, set out a partially completed project you've been working on. The suggestion is that your home is so easy to take care of that they're going to have plenty of time for hobbies.

Make use of whatever furniture you may have in storage down there, from a spare chair or end table, to the patio furniture, and set up a little conversation area. Put the chair(s) and end table together as a small sitting area.

This is really important if your neighborhood research shows that most homes in your area have a finished basement and your basement is unfinished. Set your basement up as a family room as much as possible so people may not even notice that it doesn't have drywall walls and carpeting like your competition.

To cover particularly messy areas, set up screens or portable panels. But basements are expected to be somewhat of a jumble, so don't go overboard.

The Garage or Carport

The number one thing to remember with a garage or carport is to always park your car in the garage if you can. The garage's primary purpose is storage of your car(s), and leaving it sitting in the driveway suggests there isn't enough space in the garage to hold it—which you certainly don't want to imply.

> **Experts Explain** _____
>
> "In the lower end of the market, it's fine to pack things neatly in one corner of the garage. But if your house is listed at the top end of the market, empty the garage as best you can, and paint the floor with gray cement paint so its looks like you could eat off of it! The more costly your home, the less you should see in the garage."
>
> —Barb Schwarz, author of Home Staging: The Winning Way to Sell Your House for More Money

Any car in the garage should also be washed. How you care for your car and garage is a cue to buyers of how well you care for your home—it's part of the image you are creating.

Declutter and Clean That Garage

It's perfectly fine to store boxes in your garage if there is space, but we don't recommend piling so many boxes that your car won't fit. Either store it elsewhere in your home, or offsite at a storage facility.

When cleaning, the most important part of a garage is the floor. The floor needs to be as spic-and-span as possible. That means hosing out the entire garage to get rid of dust and dirt and cleaning up any oil stains.

You should also test your garage door openers to make sure they are working well and that there is a safeguard that prevents the door from closing completely if something is blocking its path. The last thing you want to have happen is to have a buyer's child get hurt because the garage door didn't stop in time for them to get out of the way.

Also make sure that any doors leading outside or into the home are accessible and not blocked by bikes, boxes, or other belongings. Buyers will want to test the door and explore what's outside the garage—don't make it difficult.

Staging Snafu

If you own an RV or camper, don't park it anywhere near your home. Ask a friend or relative if you can park it in their driveway while your home is on the market. Campers make the home look smaller, block the sightline to the yard and building, and can be very distracting to buyers, who may not be able to envision the property without it there.

Styling Your Garage

There is really very little to do to style a garage beyond parking your clean car(s) inside, and making sure it is clean, neat, and organized. That's what buyers want to see.

But when deciding where to store packing boxes—either garage or basement—choose the space that is not as nice as the other. For instance, if the inside of your garage is nicer than your basement, store your boxes in the basement. Show off your best space.

The Attic

As with basements, attic spaces can be finished and usable as living space, or they can be unfinished and used more for storage. Whatever the condition, one of the first things you'll want to check on is its accessibility.

If you have a pull-down ladder, check it over to make sure it is sturdy and in good condition. Buyers will soon be using it, so make sure they won't be hurt when they do. Or if you have stairs, clean them off and make sure there is plenty of light, just like the basement. Some people are also uncomfortable going up into dark attics, so you'll want to do whatever you can to calm any jitters.

It really doesn't matter if the attic is finished or not, all you want to do is show the potential room to expand the home if the new buyer wanted. Or, if it's not used for expansion, you show the added storage space.

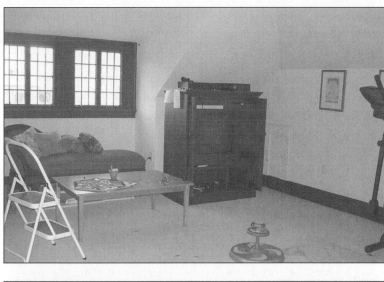

With clutter still in view, it's hard to imagine this attic as living space.

(Courtesy of Amy Ross and Beth Sammarone, The Redesign Team)

Now staged as a living or reading room, this attic shines and adds hundreds of extra square feet to this home's space (upping the perceived value).

(Courtesy of Amy Ross and Beth Sammarone, The Redesign Team)

If your attic consists of just insulation laid over ceiling boards with no real floor, consider putting down some plywood over top of the slats to create an area for storing boxes. In addition to allowing you to store some more boxes upstairs, doing so will also show the buyers what is possible up there.

If there is a floor already, vacuum and sweep to get rid of dust and dirt that can trigger allergic reactions. Air it out by opening any vents.

Just as you did in the basement, try to set up usage zones. One corner could be for storing holiday decorations and another could be for holding suitcases and travel paraphernalia, for instance.

If the attic could be used as an additional room, setting up a conversation area with extra furniture would help to drive home that idea. Treat it more like a living room than a storage closet. You want buyers to imagine the possibilities.

The Laundry Area

Today, laundry areas are located in a wide variety of places in the home, from the basement to the mudroom on the first floor to the second floor, close to the bedrooms. But because they are frequently found in the basement, we thought we would make some suggestions here for presenting your laundry room or area in the best possible light.

Most homeowners have both a washer and dryer, but not everyone has ample storage room around the appliances. The best possible scenario is shelving directly above the washer and dryer. If you have an open shelf, you'll want to line your bottles of detergent, bleach, and fabric softener neatly, with labels facing out. And if you have a cabinet with doors, organize it the same way, since you know buyers will be opening it.

It's okay if you have clothing in the laundry area, but make sure it is folded neatly and is on the shelf, not the top of the washer or dryer. Nothing should be on top of either.

Money Maker

In a pinch, a dryer is an excellent place to store things last minute. Few buyers will actually open it up to look inside.

However, you should not be in the process of washing or drying your clothing while buyers are touring your home, nor should they see any dirty laundry. You don't want any suggestion that buyers will have mundane tasks like laundry to do in their new home.

If you have an ironing board, it should be folded and hung up on the wall or put away in a closet.

Since dryers are some of the dustiest appliances around, it's a good idea to wipe down both your washer and dryer to clean them off.

Laundry areas are fairly functional spaces—you go in there to tackle a particular task and rarely for any other reason. So there should be few, if any, decorative items in the laundry area. A picture or two on the walls is okay, but nothing more.

You want the image of your laundry area to be of a well-oiled machine. Buyers see the sparkling clean appliances and the tightly organized bottles of detergent, but no sign of anything actually needing cleaning. That's perfect.

Buyers should walk away from your home impressed by how well it has been maintained, and how much possibility the extra spaces hold for them.

The Least You Need to Know

- ◆ Basements and attics don't need to be set up to indicate a particular purpose, such as bedroom or hobby space.

- ◆ Because basements are typically dark and creepy for some buyers, make yours considerably brighter by painting walls a very bright white, and the concrete floors gray.

- ◆ Large, plain rugs are a great way to establish zones for different types of usage in your basement and attic. One rug could delineate the space for TV watching, another for hobbies and crafts, and another for exercise, for example.

- ◆ Your attic, like your basement, is room to expand, from the buyer's perspective. Keep it neat and organized to allow them to imagine its potential.

- ◆ Always park your clean car in your garage, rather than in the driveway.

- ◆ Keep your laundry area tidy and never have laundry—clean or dirty—anywhere in sight.

Part 4

The Finishing Touches

What if the home you have to sell is not your typical single-family house? Don't worry, in this part we'll give you specific ideas for almost any type of property.

We'll also help you prepare for the upcoming tours of your home. Whether real estate agents, brokers, neighbors, or potential buyers are coming through, you'll be ready to impress with your exceptionally staged home.

You've worked hard to get to this point, now get ready for the compliments.

Staging the Exceptional Home

In This Chapter

- Putting buyers in a vacation mood
- Boosting investment property values
- Winning over renters
- Estate sale essentials

Seventy-five percent of all homes sold in the U.S. in 2005 were detached single-family homes, reports the National Association of Realtors. That means chances are good that you're reading this book to help make more money from the sale of your single family home. But if you happen to own one of the 25 percent of homes for sale that don't fit into the single-family category, you'll want to hear about staging techniques that can get the property off your hands faster, with more money in your pocket.

An exceptional home—meaning that it is an exception to the standard single-family home profile—can be anything from an ocean-front cottage, a hunting lodge, an off-campus building available for rent, an investment property you're ready to jettison, a place you've inherited, or a home that

Money Maker

In *Freakonomics*, the author, Steven Levitt, lists five real estate terms correlated to a higher sales price: granite, state-of-the-art, Corian, maple, and gourmet. Whenever possible use these terms to describe aspects of your home.

has been vacant for a while. And what makes them different is that they appeal to a different buyer than those searching for a single-family home.

The buyers' needs, interests, and priorities are frequently different when they're looking for a second home, or investment real estate, versus a home they'll live in eleven months out of the year. And you need to keep that in mind as you declutter, clean, repair, and stage an exceptional home. You can't approach it exactly the same way as a single family home or you may miss out on sales opportunities.

Vacation Homes

If you own a vacation home and are now readying it for sale, or for rent, there is one basic concept that should guide all you do: establish why someone would come to the area. Do they come for the fishing at the local lake? Do they come to enjoy the ocean beaches? Or is your town more popular during the winter months for skiing? What is the one reason the area is popular? That's what you want to play up in your home—you want to remind buyers why they'd want to spend time there.

Clear Out and Clean Up

First though, you'll want to take care of the basic clean up we've talked about in previous chapters. Tackle any unfinished repair projects, clear out clutter to reveal how easy it is for buyers to enjoy the space, and clean it up to emphasize how little cleaning is needed (no one likes to spend much time cleaning when they're on vacation).

Next, as you begin to stage the rooms in the home, envision who the typical buyer will be. If it's likely they'll be bringing guests with them when they use the property, you'll want to emphasize how much guest space there is. You can do that by decorating the bedrooms as guest rooms, rather than having a child's room and a home office, for instance.

Another feature vacation home buyers often want and need is storage space, especially if some of the activities include boating, with all of its paraphernalia, fishing, with all of its equipment, skiing—you get the idea. Show off the ample closet space, any benches that provide storage, as well as a loft, if there is one, or storage elsewhere on the premises, such as a boathouse or shed.

Money Maker _____

According to the National Association of Realtors, approximately 12 percent of all homes purchased in 2005 were vacation homes. Of those who purchased a second home, the most valued characteristics were: ocean, river, or lake proximity—40 percent; proximity to family members—34 percent; proximity to preferred recreational activities and proximity to their primary residence—27 percent; proximity to mountains—26 percent; proximity to a preferred vacation area—24 percent; and proximity to a job or school—17 percent.

Props Set the Stage

Finally, you can start to stage, using the primary draw to the area as your theme. For example, if antiquing is all the rage in the area and folks like to spend their weekends poking around all the antique shops, invest in a coffee table book on antiques to place on your coffee table or a bedside table.

This view of the back patio of a Florida home captures the essence of being on vacation in a warm climate.

(Courtesy of Dan Bullock, Realty Executives)

If fishing is the draw, place fishing references around the house to help buyers picture how much fun they'll have fishing there. That could include a large framed map of the lake on which your home sits, on the wall. Some fishing poles hanging in the closet can be another subtle reminder. Perhaps a map of secret fishing holes sitting out on the dining room table will catch anglers' eyes. Props help buyers feel how much they'll enjoy being there, enjoying whatever amenities they're interested in.

You can apply the same ideas to other sports, too. A charming ski chalet near a popular mountain would benefit by placing skis in the closet or even hanging skis as a piece of art on a large wall. Display a book about the top ski destinations on the coffee table or even a display of ski patrol awards on the wall. You don't want to go overboard with your tchotchkes, but a few mementos help set the mood (the buying mood, that is).

Staging Snafu

A handful of strategically placed reminders of the area's amenities is smart, but don't make your home a themed house by decorating it entirely with seashells, for example, or boating décor. The props should be subtle. Don't hit them over the head repeatedly with them.

Usually the rule is to put your collections away, but that doesn't apply as much here. If your collections have to do with the activity of the area, such as skiing or swimming or hunting, for instance, you'll want to proudly display them. Don't go overboard, however. You want to sell the experience of being in the area, but still keep the space clutter-free.

If you have a cabin or hunting camp, excite buyers about the recreational opportunities.

(Courtesy of Julie Dana, The Home Stylist)

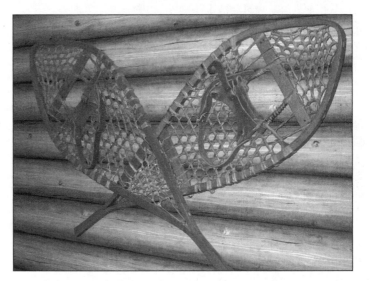

Reeling in Renters

If you're staging your vacation home to attract potential tenants, the same rules apply to decorating, but you'll want to be sure your renters feel they're getting a good value for their money.

If yours is near a beach, but not on it, provide a map to the waterfront, to emphasize how close it is. Or if you're on a lake, a diagram to the public boat launch is also useful.

Don't stow away all the accoutrements your family enjoys if renters will be allowed to use them, too. While you might not want to allow renters to borrow your brand new motor boat, letting them see and use your grill; boats, such as a canoe or sunfish; fishing gear; sunbathing gear, such as floatation devices; bikes; and other fun toys will show them the value of renting your place—with all the extras—versus the one down the road that is stripped down.

Rental Properties

When you own a property that you primarily rent, the purpose of staging is to make the space look as expensive as possible to justify the (higher) rent—the more luxurious the place feels, the more money you can charge.

Do Your Homework

Before you put your property on the market, research what comparable places in your area are renting for. Look at the total square footage, number of bedrooms and bathrooms, area of town, and any extras that would distinguish theirs from yours. That should give you a general range to work within.

To be able to rent your place at the high end of the pricing scale, you'll need to stage it so that it meets your target audience's needs better than other properties in the area. That means playing up all it offers and compensating for anything it doesn't offer, such as if your place is a little further from campus, or you don't have a backyard pool. Possible ways to get around those negatives could include having a map of the campus shuttle on hand, demonstrating how quickly students can get to class without even having to walk, or providing a pass to the local swim club for families who really want to be able to enjoy a pool.

It all comes down to matching your property to the specific needs and wants of your potential renters.

Who's Your Audience?

The type of property you own and the area in which it is located will determine who your typical renter is, and what their needs are. You can't assume that renters will be just like you. In fact, they could fit any number of profiles, including:

- **Executive families.** If you live in an area that is home to the headquarters of a major corporation or institution, it's possible that senior personnel may come into the area for short periods of time on assignment. Or they may move quickly and need a place to stay while they house hunt. Sometimes the corporation may pay the housing cost, but the family's main concern is finding a safe, homey space to settle short-term. And, of course, that short-term stay could very well become long-term if they like your property.

- **Weekday commuters.** Employees who prefer to live in one area but work in another are a possible source of rental income at either end—for weekend getaways or weekday accommodations.

- **Flight attendants.** Another type of worker who may want a place to come home to, but which they'll need only every few days, are flight attendants. They may be mostly concerned with price, accessibility to work, and quiet, so they can sleep any hour of the day, depending on their schedule.

- **Students.** If you have property in a college town, where students are prime rental candidates, your staging goal is to emphasize how carefree and convenient it is to live there, rather than trying to make the space feel luxurious.

- **Vacationers.** As we described previously, vacation renters are another population of folks interested in a short-term stay away from home.

Experts Explain

"Countless times I have recorded a more timely sale at a much closer to (if not at full) asking price when the decorating and furnishings were found attractive by the buyers. I have seen couples walk into a place and watch the wife turn to her husband, nudge him with an elbow lovingly, and say 'I want this one!' As long as the listing price was somewhat 'realistic,' these transactions came together quickly and had far fewer problems handling the 'bumps' along the way towards a successful closing."

—Dan Bullock, Realty Executives

Decorate for Them

Once you've determined who your most likely renter is, you'll want to declutter, clean, and stage to showcase how well the space meets their particular needs.

Of course, it's always best to show the place with furniture in it, even if the furniture isn't staying. Seeing objects in a room helps renters, and buyers, get perspective, to evaluate whether their belongings will fit.

Depending on whether you're trying to appeal to a senior corporate manager and her family, or an undergraduate college student, stage your home for luxury or function and convenience, respectively, to get the most money.

Estate Sale

If you've recently inherited a property, or are trying to help someone close to you sell a property that is no longer needed, you may have quite a bit of work on your hands. An estate sale generally means that the owner has passed away or has moved to a nursing home after many years in the same home and is not involved in getting the property ready for sale. It's also often a difficult time for everyone emotionally.

Getting Into the Cycle

For every neighborhood, there is a generational cycle. Some neighborhoods are made up mainly of older couples whose children have grown and moved out of the nest. Other neighborhoods have turned over and now consist primarily of newlyweds and young families. And others are in flux, with a mix of old and young.

Look at the composition of the neighborhood to get a sense of where properties are in the cycle. That will tell you who your buyer is likely to be and how you should stage the home to appeal to that audience.

The Work to Be Done

With estate homes, the decluttering and cleaning process is generally a much bigger part of the process. Most need repairs and remodeling, especially if the owner has been there for a long period of time without having upgraded along the way.

Some of the bigger projects you may need to tackle include:

- **Carpeting.** Carpeting that is old and worn should be the first thing to go. Getting rid of it and replacing it with newer neutral carpet, or hardwoods, also helps freshen the air, since carpeting is where a lot of odors are trapped.

- **Linoleum.** Kitchen and bathroom floors also frequently need ripping up and replacing, especially if the style harkens back to an older era. Of course, if you find hardwoods underneath, think seriously about having them refinished, assuming they're in decent shape, instead of recovering them. Hardwood floors = money.

- ◆ **Counters.** Again, in the kitchen and bathroom, countertops are generally reminiscent of past decades and need updating.

- ◆ **Wall color.** Cleaning and repainting walls a neutral color is a must-do, as is removing any wallpaper.

- ◆ **Lighting.** Replacing light fixtures that are not considered stylish any more can be worth the investment. This might include bathroom lights, overhead fixtures, and chandeliers, for instance.

- ◆ **Repairs.** Look for anything that doesn't work, or might need a touch-up.

But don't style the home to your own taste—style it to meet the needs of buyers, according to the stage of the neighborhood.

If you expect young families to be checking out the home, style the extra bedrooms as children's rooms. If you think older couples may be more interested, convert those bedrooms to a guest bedroom and an office or craft room. Match the features to your potential buyer.

A Flipped House

If you bought a property with the hopes of fixing it up and reselling it fast for a profit, how much money you put into updating it should be determined by who you expect to sell to.

The same rules of staging apply whether the home needed a lot of work or just some cosmetic improvements. You'll want to buy the most expensive-looking upgrades you can afford, which doesn't necessarily mean it needs to cost a lot. But who your buyer is will dictate how much of an upgrade you need at all.

For instance, a single family home may require modern appliances, fixtures, and style, while student housing may only require the basics. You might put in a granite countertop in an upscale family neighborhood, but the appeal might be lost on college students who are perfectly happy with laminate. Don't spend more than you have to.

Staging Snafu

It can be tricky to make money flipping homes because buyers notice if you skimped on the workmanship. If you decide to tackle any improvements yourself, make sure you do a job at least equivalent to someone you would hire.

Vacant

Surprisingly, vacant homes of any type are the hardest to sell. Lacking personality and perspective, buyers can't assess the size or potential of the rooms.

Cheap Furniture Outlets

If you need to take all your furniture with you when you move out, or you're helping to stage an estate home and need inexpensive pieces of furniture, here are some potential sources:

Money Maker

If you're moving out of a home you intend to sell, try to plan ahead to leave some furniture behind. A few chairs, tables, and a bed can make the difference between a quick sale and a long time on the market.

- ◆ **Garage sale.** One of the cheapest places to get furniture, garage sales are great, but they take some time to cruise.

- ◆ **Flea market.** You can check out hundreds of vendors in a short period of time, picking up basic pieces of furniture as well as interesting accessories for little money.

- ◆ **Consignment stores.** If you have a used furniture store nearby, you can often find cheap chairs and tables there.

- ◆ **Thrift shop.** Stores run by organizations like Goodwill and the Salvation Army can be excellent sources for inexpensive staging tools.

- ◆ **Auctions.** Household auctions are another great source of inexpensive furniture.

- ◆ **Family and friends.** Perhaps the best place to find furniture—and it may not cost you a dime—is asking family and friends to borrow their cast-offs.

Of course, you don't need to borrow enough furniture to fill a home, just enough to set the stage for buyers, to give them a sense of what's possible in each of the rooms.

Basic Furniture Requirements

While more is better, the basic pieces of furniture you need to properly stage a home include:

Money Maker

One of the secrets of home staging professionals is the use of outdoor camping beds as beds in vacant homes. They come in various sizes and set up on four legs, and with a pillow and comforter on it, you have a beautiful bed.

- Living room—a chair, end table, and lamp

- Bedroom—at least one bedroom needs to have a bed

- Dining room—a table of some kind, which can be fashioned from a card table or outdoor plastic table, with a tablecloth covering it

Within each room, use the furniture you have to direct attention to focal points that set the mood— a mini-vignette. For instance, in the living room by the fireplace, place a chair and add a nice pillow and drape a soft throw over the top to set the tone for the room—relaxation.

In the dining room, add a good-sized bouquet of flowers to the table and chairs and you're done.

One little extra touch will make the difference between bland and bought.

This room has some pleasing features—the built-ins, the fireplace, the neutral walls— but they're overshadowed by the lack of any furniture.

(Courtesy of Jennifer Keener, Amazing Transformations)

By adding just a chair, some artwork over the fireplace, and some accessories, such as a small plant, the room is cozy and much more appealing.

(Courtesy of Jennifer Keener, Amazing Transformations)

Historic Home

Another challenging type of home is the historic property, which may have prohibitions on any kinds of change to the exterior appearance. Sometimes even the interior structure can't be modified. But buyers willing to consider such homes are often very interested in the historical significance of the property and may be willing to overlook any restrictions.

For instance, if a well-known historical figure once lived in the home, research all you can about the individual and create a package of information in a binder or folder about the person and the house.

If there have been any magazine articles about the home, try and request a back issue and lay the article open for potential buyers to see.

Or if the home was built by an important architect, place a coffee table book on the architect or the style out in the living room.

The Least You Need to Know

◆ Exceptional homes are properties that are not single-family homes, currently making up 25 percent of the U.S. real estate market.

◆ The key with staging vacation homes is to help buyers imagine the experience they will have enjoying the home. Using props to emphasize the area's amenities, such as fishing rods in the closet or a coffee table book on ski resorts, helps set the stage.

◆ With rental units, it's important to determine the renter's primary needs and then stage to match that. An executive family's requirements will be much different than a group of college students, for example.

◆ Estate homes being sold following the death of a loved one often requires a significant amount of decluttering, cleaning, and updating to become sellable.

◆ Vacant homes are the most difficult to sell, because buyers can't accurately gauge how large the rooms are without furniture in them. The solution is to borrow or buy cheaply a few key pieces of furniture to dress up the rooms.

◆ Historic homes, with all their restrictions, may still appeal to history buffs. Gather all the information you can about the home's historic significance and make it available to anyone touring the home.

Chapter 18

It's Show Time

In This Chapter

- ◆ Making your home as photogenic as possible
- ◆ Prepping for an open house
- ◆ Encouraging neighborhood buzz
- ◆ Key styling tricks

Once your home has been decluttered, cleaned, and staged, it's time to show it off to potential buyers. Whether you're having a public open house, a broker and agent open house, or you're taking appointments to show it, there are a number of finishing touches you'll want to bestow on each room to impress all who tour your home.

Photos Worth More Than 1,000 Words

Even before you start final preparations for public showings of your home, you need to put your best foot forward in the photos your agent (if you're using one) or you need to take. In addition to needing an exterior photo for the one page flyer you'll hand out to prospective buyers, sharing photos of the interior of your home is now very common on real estate websites.

Buyers can take an initial peek at homes for sale through their local online multiple listing service (MLS) to identify potential properties to tour in person and to eliminate others from consideration. Those home photos can make or break a sale right up front, even before a buyer has seen the property, because if the home looks unkempt, outdated, and/or dirty from a distance, few buyers will take the time to take a closer look.

Experts Explain

According to the National Association of Realtors (NAR), in 1995 just 2 percent of home buyers used the Internet to look at homes. By 2005 that percent had risen to 77, an indicator of how important a home's online image is.

The photos of your home need to show it in the best possible light, in the hopes of getting online buyers excited about seeing it as quickly as possible, before someone else snaps it up. Here are some things to keep in mind as you start shooting.

Taking the "After" Photos

Remember the photos you took in Chapter 2? Those were your "before" photos—what your home looked like before you began the home staging process. They gave you a better sense of what visitors saw when they walked into each room and helped you spot opportunities for improvement—the pile of papers teetering on the side of your desk, the stained corner of your ceiling that needed painting, and the cluttered kitchen countertop full of appliances and dishes.

Photographs are helpful because they are so objective. They show us exactly what each room looks like to others—highlighting areas needing attention that we have grown so used to. Photos make such overlooked areas obvious.

Of course, all that work is behind us and your rooms no longer resemble what you saw in those "before" photos. Although you may not want to be reminded of all the work you just did, it's time to take those photos out of the box or envelope where you've been storing them—you'll need to refer to them when taking your "after" photos.

Return to the Scene of the Crime

When taking your new "after" photos of the rooms in your home, try your best to duplicate the location, position, and perspective you used when you took your "before" photos. If you stood on a chair to be sure your fireplace stood out in a photo, do that again. Or if you stood on your staircase looking into your dining room, try to find the same stair for your "after" photo.

The same goes for your exterior shots—get as far away from your home to take the photo as you were when you took the "before" photo.

Why does this matter? Because matching the two sets of photos as closely as possible serves two purposes. First, and most important, the new photos will help you spot any remaining trouble areas. What will buyers notice first in each room? Is that what you intended? And second, the photos will confirm the progress you've made in sprucing up your space. If you ever wondered whether all your time and energy was well spent in staging your home, these latest photos will certainly show you how worthwhile your effort was.

Staging Snafu

When taking a series of images of your home, be as comprehensive as possible. Leaving out an important vantage point—such as a shot of the front of the home, or the kitchen—will leave buyers assuming the home is ugly and the kitchen a wreck. Don't skip an important room. Buyers will notice and may cross your home off their list of properties to tour.

Oh, the Places They'll Go

Besides confirming what a great job you did in staging your home to sell, you'll use the new photos in several ways:

- **Flyer.** Most real estate agents prepare a marketing brochure or flyer with a photo of the front of your home front and center on the first page.

- **Multiple listing service.** If you'll be listing your home with an agent, you need an electronic version of that same frontal view of your home.

- **Agent's website.** Some real estate agents have their own websites, or their agency's have a website, which is another opportunity to show off your home with a photo or series of photos.

- **Personal website.** Some sellers elect to create a separate website devoted to selling their home, which features a front view as well as several interior shots. If you'll be selling it yourself, as a for sale by owner (FSBO) listing, you'll still want to either host it on your own site or on a FSBO site.

Taking Control

If you're working with a real estate agent, expect the agent to offer to—or expect to—take the photo he or she will use to market your home. This is standard procedure, but you may want to be an active participant in the photo shoot, rather than leaving the whole process to the agent. You have a lot more riding on the sale of your home than your agent, so consider either offering to take the photo yourself, or offering to serve as a photo assistant—moving furniture, opening curtains, turning on lights as needed—to the agent behind the camera.

Another reason you may want to have the images loaded on your camera, and not your agent's, is that you may want to do some of your own marketing and having the image in your possession may make life easier. Be sure and get it to your agent ASAP, however, since he or she needs it, too.

Secrets of Stunning Pictures

The "before" pictures you took of your home were for your own personal use and not for public consumption, so it really didn't matter if they weren't perfect. No one else was going to see them anyway. Now, however, many people will see the photos—many potential buyers—so you'll want to take extra care to photograph your home looking its absolute best. The following are some tips for getting the best results possible.

It's the Equipment

It's amazing what a difference a higher end camera can make when taking photographs. That doesn't mean that you should rush out and buy one, of course, but see if you can rent or borrow some components to give your existing camera a boost. Some extra accessories that can enhance your photos include:

- **Wide angle lens.** If you don't often have to take photos of entire rooms, ask your agent or the broker's photographer if you can borrow their wide angle lens to take interior shots of your rooms. Rather than being limited to photographing a portion of a room, a wide angle lens captures nearly the entire space in one image.

- **Good flash.** Since bright rooms are much easier to sell than dark and dingy ones, borrowing or renting a strong flash bulb unit will be well worth the investment.

◆ **Tripod.** If you're taking the photos yourself and are doing double-duty as photo assistant and cameraperson, setting the camera up on a tripod can save you a lot of time and improve the quality of the images.

Money Maker

One of the best places to find low-cost photography equipment rentals is a local darkroom or community photography studio. You may be able to borrow all the equipment you need over a weekend for less than it costs to buy a good flash. If you don't have a community darkroom, check with your local recreation center, local high school, or adult education center.

Wait for a Sunny Day

Believe it or not, buyers prefer homes that are light and airy. They like sunny spaces. So when taking photos of your home, wait for a sunny day to ensure you get the maximum amount of light possible in your home. Waiting a day or two for better weather will have a dramatic impact on the outcome of your photo session. The sunnier it is outside, the more sunshine that can flow through into your home, making it that much more bright and appealing.

Once your sunny day arrives, approach each room as a canvas. You want to tell a story without distraction. That means you may need to move some furniture around. No one said you have to leave your furniture in place exactly the way you use it everyday. If an upholstered chair is blocking your view of the fireplace, move it out of the room. Or if your sofa is taking up a lot of space in the bottom of your camera view, step up on a chair for a better, unobstructed view.

On top of moving extraneous furniture out of the way, you'll also want to be sure you have no people or pets in the photos. Buyers want to imagine themselves in your home, which is hard to do if you show someone working away in your home office, or taking a nap on your sofa. Since many people have allergies, showing your beloved kitty stretched out in front of the fire, or dog lounging in the sunny front window, may scare some buyers off. Better to keep them out of the picture.

Another tip for taking great photos is to focus on the room—the big picture. Try to capture as much of the room as possible in one photo. The best way to do this is to take the picture on an angle. That is, when you look through your camera's viewfinder, the corner of the room should be in the center of the image. Taking the picture on an angle provides perspective to anyone looking at the image, and offers a more interesting view than a flat wall, for example.

Showing the big picture is important, but so is showing the details. If your home features architectural details buyers may find desirable, be sure they're in the photo.

Staging Snafu

Seasonal decorations like a cornhusk scarecrow, Christmas lights, or Valentine's Day hearts are a clear giveaway to buyers that your home has been on the market for a while. The same goes for weather indicators, like snow in the photo when today's weather outside is steamy. Make sure your photos are up-to-date and free of seasonal decoration to prevent the impression your home is a difficult sell.

Money Maker

To show off the land surrounding their property, or proximity to a desirable landmark, some savvy home sellers include a link to a satellite photo of their home on their website.

That means paying special attention to include the crown molding in the dining room shot, or moving in a little closer so buyers see the ornate banister going up the stairs.

While the interior is important, the exterior shot of the front of your home will probably be the most used and most viewed. Given that, do all you can to make your home stand out.

Take the photo on a sunny day so the property looks pleasant and inviting. Make sure the front walkway or stoop is swept and clear of debris. Do some yard work before the shot if you spy weeds in your flower beds or dog droppings in the grass. All window treatments should be pulled back and blinds up in the windows so it looks lived in.

Finally, if one of the big draws of the home is the view out the back, make sure you have a photograph of that view both from the outside—perhaps from a back deck—and from the inside. Make sure buyers don't miss how special that view is.

Once you've captured every pleasing angle of your home on film or memory stick, it's time to prep for the in-person tour.

Open House Options

Although there has been some question lately regarding whether open houses are outdated, in most parts of the country open houses are still very much in evidence. Of course, there are a few negatives:

◆ **It can make you vulnerable to theft.** By opening your home to anyone coming in off the street, you're also opening yourself up to theft, by permitting strangers to take note of your belongings. Some thieves pick up what they can while in the property while others case the joint with plans to return later.

◆ **Most of your visitors are neighbors.** While it's true that many open house guests are nosy neighbors eager to get a look at the inside of your home, that's not necessarily a negative. Neighbors who are well aware of how beautiful your newly updated kitchen looks, or how fabulous your finished basement is, are more likely to rave about it to others who are house hunting.

However, the pros outweigh the cons. Here is a list of the advantages:

 Money Maker

In order for an open house to be effective at getting buyers off the fence, you need to have had potential buyers come through the home already. That means, don't hold an open house the first week your home is on the market. Wait at least until the second or third week before scheduling one.

◆ **Scheduling an open house sets an inflexible deadline for you.** Once the open house has been announced, you have a finite amount of time to get your work done, which some sellers have remarked helped push them to finish it.

◆ **Encouraging interested buyers to get off the fence and make an offer.** If a potential buyer has come through your home and is debating whether to make an offer, hearing that an open house is scheduled is sometimes enough to push them to fill out the paperwork for fear that another buyer will become interested after seeing it.

◆ **Helping to get the word out.** Most sellers know they shouldn't expect to get an offer following an open house, but letting others tour it can certainly help spread the word about it.

Four Types of Tours

While most of us associate the words open house with a public tour of your home, there are actually four variations on the open house tour. In addition to open houses which are open to the public, there are also real estate professional open houses, during which 10 to 15 agents associated with the real estate office your own agent works in stop by at a specified hour to see the home, and a broker's open house, which multiple real estate agencies attend. Finally, there is the tour-by-appointment, which most serious buyers call to schedule.

Real Estate Professional Open House

Agents who work together in the same office often have camaraderie or a desire to help each other succeed. With that mindset, agents affiliated with your agent's office are probably more likely to ultimately sell your home. This is why it is important to impress them with your clean and stylish home.

These agents will typically stop by in a caravan of cars during a tour of between three and 10 homes in one morning. They're trying to get a sense of what's currently available, so that they can alert buyers they're working with of any properties that may meet their needs. Your challenge is to make your home as memorable as possible—so that the agents come away raving about a particular aspect. It doesn't really matter what that aspect is, as long as it's possible. Maybe yours has the professional chef's kitchen or the media room worthy of Steven Spielberg—whatever your home's best feature is, make sure it stands out to this bunch.

Broker's Open House

Second in importance among the list of open houses is the broker's open house, during which area real estate agents and brokers converge on several homes to get a sense of how saleable the property is. Since getting agents excited about your home is typically the first step to selling it, sellers in some parts of the country are going above and beyond to entice brokers to stop by. Generally that means a fancy affair involving the city's most expensive caterer.

Public Open House

As we said, most of the people who stop by a public open house, held often on a weekend afternoon, will be neighbors curious about what's behind your front door. And that's OK. Although they may not personally be in the market for a new home, they probably know someone who is and can help spread the word about your terrific space.

By Appointment Tour

When a home becomes available, buyers will frequently set an appointment through their real estate agent to tour it. They'll schedule a time to walk through it at their leisure, frequently during the week.

Sometimes, however, such appointments occur at the last minute, such as when an out-of-town buyer arrives and wants to see homes in a particular neighborhood. Those situations are frequently the most difficult to prepare for, which is why you'll want to try and keep your home in tip-top shape at all times while it's on the market.

Game Time

Whether you're expecting a knock at the door any minute, or are getting ready for an open house this weekend, there are several steps you can take to get your home ready for a tour.

The Nose Knows

As they step over the threshold into your home, buyers get an immediate whiff of how you live. Even before they start to take in the view, their nose gives them an impression of the space. To ensure that impression does not include cat pee, smoke, or menthol medication, try this:

◆ Open the windows in the front and back of the house an hour before you expect visitors and let a breeze flow through. If the air is stale or you want to get rid of lingering odors, fresh air is the best solution.

◆ Don't cook aromatic foods, such as peppers and onions, the night before an open house. Food smells spread beyond the kitchen and can be pungent.

◆ Wipe down bathrooms with pine scented disinfectant and pour a little into the toilet—but don't flush—to help reinforce the scent of clean.

The overall smell you want buyers to have is "clean."

Bring the Outside In

Beyond a clean smell, it's also helpful if buyers see small touches of nature inside. Not only do flowers and plants brighten up the space and make a positive impact, they also add to the clean and fresh aura.

◆ Buy a prestigious floral arrangement from a higher end florist to place in the entryway or in the dining room. This bouquet should make a statement, suggesting your home is as prestigious as the flowers you display. (That means no carnations or cheaper flowers.)

◆ Place individual flowers in strategic spots around the home. A single small rose in a bud vase by the bed, for instance, and a lily in a vase in the bathroom.

◆ Clear out plants on their last leg. If you have plants that you're in the process of nursing back to health, ask if you can relocate them to a neighbor while your home is for sale. Buyers want to see that everything in your home is well cared for and half-dead plants don't support that impression.

Experts Explain

We've heard from real estate professionals in some parts of the country that sellers of higher end homes are now offering buyer incentives. To speed a sale and entice buyers into committing, sellers are offering everything from a home warranty to cover all major expenses to paying property taxes for the first year to a new car. Is there any incentive you might offer to boost your home's desirability to buyers?

Lights On

Buyers like bright, sunny homes, so do your best to give them what they want.

◆ Turn on every light in your home, even during the daytime.

◆ Pull back window treatments so as not to block any sun, and pull up blinds or other shades out of the way. (The only exception to this instruction is if the window has an ugly view, such as the side of the neighbor's garage).

Valuables

Keeping in mind one of the downsides of having an open house—would-be thieves on the premises—put away anything of value, to prevent temptation. This includes:

◆ Money, credit card or bank receipts, or anything with personal information you wouldn't want falling into the wrong hands.

◆ Medications. Clear out your medicine cabinet, vanity, dresser drawer, or anywhere else you store prescriptions and relocate the medicine out of reach of thieves.

◆ Personal possessions. If something is valuable to you, it could be valuable to others and, therefore, more likely to be stolen. Take down valuable artwork, for example, small antiques that could be easily picked up, and any jewelry. If it's left sitting out, you may never see it again.

Furry Companions

Take all pets out of the house while buyers are in it. Not only will it make buyers more at ease, and more interested in lingering, it will reduce your pets' stress level. This includes:

◆ Dogs

◆ Cats

◆ Potbelly pigs

◆ Ferrets

◆ Lizards

◆ Guinea pigs

◆ Rabbits

◆ Hamsters and gerbils

◆ Snakes

◆ Turtles

◆ Spiders

◆ Birds

◆ Anything else that lives in a cage or other housing unit

The only exception is fish, as long as they are in a clean aquarium.

Last Minute Prep Work

Just before agents or potential buyers arrive, run through this final checklist:

◆ Make sure toilet seat lids are down

◆ Check that all beds are made

- Wipe down the sink and bathtub so that they are dry (they'll look cleaner)

- Scrub the kitchen sink until it sparkles

- Put on some soft contemporary music in the background. If you have music on upstairs and down, set the radio to the same station for consistency through the home.

Money Maker

Studies have shown that the more time buyers spend in your home, the more interested they become. So take steps to get visitors to slow down—put on relaxing music, offer snacks, and add a special touch in each room for them to find and appreciate.

- Check the traffic flow in each room. Will groups of people be able to walk easily to the window, or around the sofa? If not, move chairs and tables to make a wider passage area, or take extra pieces of furniture out altogether.

- Chat with your agent to make sure he or she is aware of your home's special touches, such as the second floor laundry chute, the energy efficient toilet, or built in spice rack in the kitchen. Unless you tell him or her, they can't tell buyers.

Staging Snafu

Never hold an open house in a vacant home. If you've already moved out, rent or borrow basic furniture to outfit most of the rooms. They don't need to be totally decorated, but they do need furniture. Otherwise, the tour will take all of two seconds.

Parking

Before real estate agents or brokers come through, offer parking directions that include instructions regarding which side of the street to park on, which driveway they can use, and alternate parking spots to avoid any tickets. Make sure there are no difficulties finding available parking.

Interestingly, the opposite is important for a public open house—give the appearance of lots of visitors, lots of interest, and make parking a little bit of a challenge. There's nothing worse for buyers than to approach a home they were interested in and seeing a lone car in the driveway (the real estate agent's). To avoid this, park a few cars—your own and neighbors' in the driveway or along the street.

Your Ultimate Goal

Your real estate agent will oversee the actual open house event, but your goal is to prepare your home so well that it is memorable to all who stop by. With so many other properties on the market—some just up the street from you—you want to be sure visitors walk away with a positive memory of your place.

Think about what you want your home's image—its tagline—to be. A tagline is like a slogan for your home.

Will it be "the lighthouse home," because you had your huge lighthouse collection on display in every single room? Will it be "the pink and blue home," because every room had a combination of those two colors—and only those two colors? Or will it be the "cat pee home," because of the noxious smell guests were greeted with at the door?

No, you want buyers to walk away raving about "the home with the amazing bouquet in the foyer," or recalling the pool in the backyard or "kitchen perfect for entertaining." Because that's what staging comes down to—presenting your home in its best possible light, so that buyers will immediately notice why it's so special (and be willing to pay a pretty penny to become the new owners).

The Least You Need to Know

- There are four types of open houses—real estate professional, broker, and public—as well as the "by appointment" home tour, for which you need to prepare.

- Although most of the people coming through your home during a public open house may be neighbors, that's OK, because they will help spread the word about your great property.

- Spend lots of time taking photographs of the interior and exterior of your home. A single photo of the front of your home will help buyers decide whether to take the time to tour it in person.

- Make sure the photos you take are also featured on real estate websites, where the majority of buyers are now looking for their next home.

Glossary

80/20 Rule   The 80/20 Rule (also known as the Pareto Principle) states that 20 percent of something is generally responsible for 80 percent of the results.

appraiser   A professional who estimates what your home is worth based on its location, size, and condition.

buzz   Excitement generated by an attractive, well-staged home that pushes real estate agents, neighbors, and potential buyers to tell all their friends about "this great house" they just saw. It's the equivalent of word-of-mouth marketing, but for real estate.

caulking   A slightly flexible vinyl or silicone-based substance used around fixtures, such as bathtubs, to prevent water from seeping underneath.

chair rail   A line of trim applied to the wall at approximately hip height—where the top of a chair would meet the wall—often used in dining rooms or as a way to separate wallpaper and paint, or two colors of paint.

charger   A decorative plate that you set your dinner plate on. They come in solid colors, generally metallic.

comparables   Homes in your area that have recently been sold and are very similar to your home's size, number of bedrooms, age, and features. Comparing your home to these properties helps you gauge its market value.

feng shui   The ancient Chinese art of placement that brings harmony to your shelter and assists in the flow of chi, the life force/spirit.

grout   A rigid type of mortar that goes in between tiles and seals them in place.

major remodeling   Structural and mechanical in nature, meaning that the shape or structure of the home may be changed, such as by finishing the attic or revising the core systems, for example by adding central air conditioning.

marketing   All the work done to persuade a buyer to make an offer, including promotional activities, listing materials, and how the home is presented.

molding   Strips of trim applied to the edges of walls, doorways, and ceilings, as a decorative element. Crown molding, for example, is used at the top of walls, abutting the ceiling.

multiple listing system (MLS)   The local database of real estate for sale within a geographic area. Generally speaking, only real estate agents can post or list properties on the system, but anyone can view the contents on the Internet.

on trend   A style that is current in fashion; it's up-to-date.

personal property   Property on the premises that goes with the homeowner.

priority   Placing a greater importance on some activities than others, based on the potential benefit of each.

sight line   The view your eyes have of a room. If you can see everything in the room, the sight line is unobstructed, but if something gets in your way, such as a large plant or piece of furniture, your sight line is blocked.

staging   Preparing your home to sell by accentuating its advantages and eliminating or reducing the perceived negatives. Results are often a quicker sale for more money than expected.

tchotchke (pronounced "chatch-kee")   The little knick-knacks, bric-a-brac, and mementos that tend to multiply over time and can give a room a cluttered look just by their presence.

up-side potential   The possibility that you will receive more than your asking price for your home. The opposite is the down-side, which is the risk you'll have to reduce the asking price in order for the home to sell.

vignette   A decorative grouping of accessories, usually in sets of three items. One is usually tall, one is medium height, and one is small, and they don't have to be the same. A clock, candle, and book, for example, could work well together.

virtual tour   Being able to tour a particular home visually by looking at photos or streaming video online at a real estate website.

Staging Checklist

To make it easier to spot areas of your property that still need staging and attention, here is a handy checklist.

Don't be discouraged by the length of this checklist—it's meant to help you keep track of what you've already done, as well as remind you of what still needs to be tackled. But nowhere does it say that you have to attempt to do everything yourself. Some activities you probably already do on a regular basis, so you can check them off right now. Other areas may require extra help, such as friends, family, or a hired handyman. Consider putting codes next to the activities you've delegated to help keep track of who's doing what.

This checklist is meant more as a friendly reminder than anything else, with a goal of helping you get more money when you sell your home.

Curb Appeal

- ❏ Front yard cleared of debris, including toys and sports equipment
- ❏ Lawn weeded and trimmed
- ❏ Yard and driveway edged
- ❏ Shrubs and trees trimmed to allow clear visibility of doors and windows
- ❏ Path to front door clearly visible
- ❏ Front door painted
- ❏ Siding cleaned
- ❏ Paint touched up where necessary
- ❏ Lawn ornaments or holiday decorations in storage
- ❏ Trash cans out of sight
- ❏ House number easily visible from road

Garage or Car Port

- ❏ Car inside
- ❏ Tools organized
- ❏ Floor clean
- ❏ Clutter removed

Entryway

❏ Holes in walls spackled and repainted

❏ Odors eliminated

❏ Lighting sufficient for nighttime tours

❏ Area rug down

❏ Mirrors and picture frames dusted and glass cleaned

❏ Personal mail and papers stored

❏ Hall closet clean and half empty

Kitchen

❏ Kitchen counters cleared and cleaned

❏ Countertops replaced if dated

❏ Cabinet hardware replaced if dated

❏ Cabinets/cupboards cleaned and half empty

❏ Contents of cabinets organized

❏ Drawers organized and half empty

❏ Fronts of refrigerator and cabinets cleared and cleaned

❏ Clutter stored away or tossed

❏ Floors scrubbed and waxed

❏ Scatter rugs removed

❏ Stove hood cleaned and degreased

Bathrooms and Powder Rooms

❏ Walls painted

❏ Cabinets painted

❏ Counter surfaces clear of clutter and clean

❏ Cabinets organized and half empty

❏ Makeup and personal items condensed

❏ Shower curtain replaced

❏ New towels purchased

❏ New coordinating bathroom rug purchased

❏ Toilet, tub, shower, and sink cleaned

❏ Floor scrubbed or shampooed

❏ Tile areas recaulked or regrouted

Formal Living Room and Family Room

❏ Clutter removed and stored or tossed

❏ Family photos removed

❏ Trophies and collections stored

❏ Walls and ceiling painted

❏ Ceiling checked for signs of water damage

❏ Furniture (re)arranged

❏ Rugs shampooed

❏ Fireplace clean with new logs in place

❏ Windows cleaned

❏ Window treatments cleaned, dusted, or removed

❏ Wood furniture polished and upholstery steam cleaned

❏ Lamps and chandeliers dusted and cleaned

❏ New, high wattage day-light bulbs placed in lamps

❏ Fresh flowers in place

Den, Home Office, or Guest Room

❏ Clutter removed and stored or tossed

❏ Family photos removed

❏ Trophies and collections stored

❏ Walls and ceiling painted

❏ Ceiling checked for signs of water damage

❏ Furniture (re)arranged

❏ Rugs shampooed

❏ Fireplace clean with new logs in place

❏ Windows cleaned

❏ Window treatments cleaned, dusted, or removed

❏ Wood furniture polished and upholstery steam cleaned

❏ Lamps and chandeliers dusted and cleaned

❏ New, high wattage day-light bulbs placed in lamps

❏ Fresh flowers in place

Dining Room

- ❏ Table leaves removed and table condensed
- ❏ Table cleared and clean
- ❏ Wall paint a neutral color
- ❏ Items removed from top of china cabinet or bookshelf
- ❏ Chairs pushed in
- ❏ Cabinets or buffets cleared and simple
- ❏ Extra furniture in storage
- ❏ Placemat and napkins in place

Master Bedroom

- ❏ Clutter removed and stored or tossed
- ❏ Wall paint a neutral color
- ❏ Last season's clothing in storage
- ❏ Personal belongings and toiletries stowed away
- ❏ Carpet shampooed
- ❏ Bedding freshly laundered, including pillows
- ❏ Bed made
- ❏ Closets clean and half empty

Master Bathroom

- ❏ Walls painted
- ❏ Cabinets painted
- ❏ Counter surfaces clear of clutter and clean

❏ Cabinets organized and half empty

❏ Makeup and personal items condensed

❏ Shower curtain replaced

❏ New towels purchased

❏ New coordinating bathroom rug purchased

❏ Toilet, tub, shower, and sink cleaned

❏ Floor scrubbed or shampooed

❏ Tile areas recaulked or regrouted

Additional Bedrooms

❏ Clutter removed and stored or tossed

❏ Last season's clothing in storage

❏ Décor neutral

❏ Personal belongings and toiletries stowed away

❏ Posters, artwork, and stuffed animals removed

❏ Carpet shampooed

❏ Bedding freshly laundered, including pillows

❏ Bed made

❏ Closets clean and half empty

Basement and Attic

❏ Clutter removed

❏ Belongings in boxes, stacked neatly

❏ Floor clean

❏ Odors eliminated

Timeline Estimator

How long will it take to stage your home for sale?

Take this fun quiz about the various areas of your home and find out how long it will take to get your home in top shape for sale.

Declutter	
I am a minimalist. I don't have any clutter.	1 point
I have a few items I need to remove.	2 points
I have clutter that I keep in check but barely.	3 points
I have clutter and lots of it in each room.	4 points
Clean	
I am fanatical about cleanliness all the time.	1 point
I thoroughly clean each week. I'll spring clean.	2 points
I clean occasionally. Don't always major clean.	3 points
I probably need a professional cleaning crew.	4 points

continues

continued

Repair	
I meticulously keep my house maintained.	1 point
I have a couple small projects to do.	2 points
I have one major project that needs work.	3 points
I have major repairs in several areas.	4 points
Curb Appeal	
I get awards for gardening and house appearance.	1 point
I have a few stray weeds and I need to mulch.	2 points
I need to paint my trim and cut foliage.	3 points
I need to paint the outside of my house.	4 points
Inside paint	
I have all cream or neutral paint. No wallpaper.	1 point
I need to repaint one room.	2 points
I need to repaint/remove wallpaper in some rooms.	3 points
I know most of my rooms need to be painted.	4 points
Furniture Arrangements and Style	
I am confident that there is not much to change.	1 point
I have slight tweaking of room layouts.	2 points
I need to remove some furniture and add style.	3 points
I know I need a furniture and style overhaul.	4 points

Your Score

Add up your points and let's see where you stand.

If you have 6 to 8 points: You should be proud. You have not much to do to get your house in top shape to sell. It will take you only 1 or 2 days to get ready to put your home on the market.

If you have between 9 and 15 points: You have some tweaking to do. With small projects and a little alteration you home can be ready in only 3 to 5 days of work.

If you have between 16 and 20 points: You know you have some work to do. You will need to make some changes before your home can be on the market. It should take you 6 to 14 days to get your home ready to sell for top dollar.

If you have 21 to 24 points: You know you have major work to do for your house to be salable. With some elbow grease and maybe a professional tradesman, you can have your home ready in 15 to 30 days.

Resources

If you'd like more information about home staging, or about other aspects of the real estate sales process, here are some useful books, magazines, and websites to help.

Books

Berges, Steve. *101 Cost Effective Ways to Increase the Value of Your Home.* Chicago: Dearborn Trade Publishing, 2004.

> A very easy-to-understand book on changes you can make to your house to increase its value.

Christian, Vicki, ed. *Designed to Sell: Smart Ideas that Pay Off!* Des Moines: Meredith Books, 2006.

> A book based on the popular HGTV show by the same name showing specific rooms and budgets.

Glink, Ilyce R. *50 Simple Steps You Can Take to Sell Your Home Faster and for More Money In Any Market.* New York: Three Rivers Press, 2003.

> In addition to tips for getting your home ready to sell, this book goes further into other marketing and pricing issues.

Lankarge, Vicki. *How to Increase the Value of Your Home*. New York: McGraw-Hill, 2005.

> This helpful book gives budget-conscious techniques and ideas that will make your home worth much more. If you are thinking about selling or remodeling, check this book first.

Schwarz, Barb, et al. *Home Staging: The Winning Way to Sell Your House for More Money*. Hoboken: Wiley, 2006.

> This book describes staging techniques as well as exploring the staging profession.

Webb, Martha and Zackheim, Sarah Parsons. *Dress Your House for Success: 5 Fast, Easy Steps to Selling your House, Apartment, or Condo for the Highest Possible Price*. New York: Three Rivers Press, 1997.

> Quick reference guide to prepping your house for the market with many nice tips for each room.

Magazines

Better Homes and Gardens
www.bhg.com

Domino
www.dominomag.com

Home
www.homemag.com

InStyle Home
www.instyle.com

Websites

www.homegain.com

A site designed to help you assess the value of your home. Also contains additional resources regarding staging and getting ready to move.

www.InteriorRedesignDirectory.com

A directory of home stagers and redesigners organized by states.

www.moving.com

A site all about moving and packing, with tips for safely and securely prepping your valuables for transportation across town or across the country.

www.OneDayDecorating.com

An internationally known training program for home staging and interior redesign professionals.

www.realtor.org

The National Association of Realtors provides research and information about the real estate industry.

www.stagedhomes.com

A comprehensive resource on the staging industry. It offers statistics on the industry as well as listings of Accredited Staging Professionals.

Index

Numbers

15 second rule, 84
80/20 rule, (Pareto Principle), 38

A

accent colors, 88-89
accent pillows, 127
accessories
    bathrooms, 183-184
    bedrooms, 172-173
    curb appeal
        adornments, 94-95
        house numbers, 93
        landscaping, 96-99
        lighting, 95
        mailboxes, 93
        pets, 96
        welcome mats, 94
    decluttering, 43
    kitchens
        adding, 153
        removing, 153-155
    vacation homes, 229-230
Accredited Staging
    Professionals (ASP), 4
additions, 79
adornments for outside, 94-95
agent websites, 241
airborne safety issues
    asbestos, 70
    lead paint, 69
    mold, 69
    radon, 70
    smoke detectors, 69
air conditioning, 71

aluminum wiring, 72
amenities, 13-14
appliances, 76, 144, 149
appointment open houses, 247
appraisals, 12-13
architects, 80, 85
arranging
    bedrooms, 168-169
    dining rooms, 135
    rental properties, 232
asbestos, 70
ASP (Accredited Staging
    Professionals), 4
assessing homes
    before pictures, 17-19
    smells, 19-20
attics, 220-222
audience for rental properties, 231-232

B

back doors, 114-115
basements
    cleaning, 215-216
    decluttering, 215-216
    finished, 215
    lighting, 216-217
    living zones, 217
    remodeling, 79
    smells, 216
    spaciousness, 216-217
    styles, 218-219
    unfinished, 214
bathrooms
    accessories, 183-184
    cleaning, 59-60, 181
    decluttering, 179-180

powder rooms, 186
    remodeling, 77-78
    repairs
        counters, 177
        fans, 178
        floors, 177
        grout/caulking, 178
        walls, 176-177
    spaciousness, 181-182
    spa image, 182-184
bathtubs, 78
bedcovers, 171-172
bedrooms
    accessories, 172-173
    arranging, 168-169
    bedcovers, 171-172
    cleaning, 163-164
    decluttering, 164
    floors, 162
    focal points, 158-159
    furniture, 160
    guest, 173
    lighting, 162, 165-166
    master bedrooms, 161, 196
    paint, 162
    purpose, 158
    repairs, 162
    secondary, 161
    spaciousness, 166
    staging example, 160-161
    storage, 167
    styles, 170
before pictures, 17-19
benefits
    cleaning, 54
    decluttering
        buyer's vision, 39
        hiding personal issues, 39

highlighting features, 38
reducing distractions, 38
spaciousness, 38
time saver, 40
staging, 6, 7
    buyer preferences, aiding, 4
    competitive advantages, 4
    objectivity, 5
blinds, 56
bookcases, 126
bricklayers, 80
broker open houses, 246
budgets, 24-25
    calculating, 25-26
    entryways, 105
    examples, 26
        under $1,000, 26-27
        under $4,000, 27
        under $8,000, 28
    room priorities, 29-31
buyers
    preferences, 4
    visualizing themselves in home, 39

C

cabinets, 74
calculating budgets, 25-26
campers, 220
carbon monoxide detectors, 69
carpenters, 80
carpeting, 79
carpet installers, 80
carports
    cleaning, 219
    decluttering, 219
    styles, 220
caulking bathrooms, 178
ceilings, 55-56
cement workers, 80

Century 21 website, 14
ceramic tiles, 75
china cabinets, 137
cleaning
    basements, 215-216
    bathrooms, 59-60, 181
    bedrooms, 163-164
    benefits, 54
    blinds, 56
    ceilings, 55-56
    closets, 192
    dining rooms, 134
    entryways, 106
    estate homes, 233
    fireplaces, 57
    floors, 57-58
    furniture, 57
    garages, 219
    hallways, 112
    home offices, 204
    kitchens, 58-59
        appliances, 149
        countertops, 151
        hanging pot racks/tools, 152
        sinks, 149
        trashcans, 151
    living rooms, 121
    nontoxic alternatives, 61
    outside, 60-61
    pet areas, 60
    rental properties, 232
    stairways, 112
    supplies, 47
    walls, 56-57
    windows, 55
    woodwork, 56
closets
    cleaning, 192
    coat, 197
    decluttering, 191-192
    half-full, 188
    hall, 197
    home offices, 205

kitchen pantries, 193
    lighting, 192
    linen, 194
    master bedroom, 196
    perfectionism, 193
    purpose, 188
    repairs, 190
    spaciousness, 198-199
clothes, 46
coat closets, 197
coffee tables, 127
Coldwell Banker website, 14
colors of houses, 87-89
comparing homes, 15
    neighborhood lifecycles, 16-17
    standards, 16
competitive advantages, 4
competitors
    comparisons, 15
        neighborhood lifecycles, 16-17
        standards, 16
    impressions, 14-15
comprehensive photographs, 241
concrete professionals, 80
contractors, 80
controlling photographs, 242
counters
    bathrooms, 177
    estate homes, 234
    kitchens, 74
        decluttering/cleaning, 151
        repairing, 145-146
creativity, 204
curb appeal
    15 second rule, 84
    adornments, 94-95
    decks, 92
    defined, 83
    doors, 89-91
    driveways, 85

house color, 87-88
house numbers, 93
landscaping, 96-99
lighting, 95
mailboxes, 93
pets, 96
ponds/water fountains, 92
pools, 92
porches, 92
prioritizing, 29
roof, 89
sidewalks, 86-87
trim/accent color, 88-89
welcome mats, 94

D

dead trees, 98
decks, 92
decluttering, 36-38
    80/20 rule, (Pareto
        Principle), 38
    accessories, 43
    basements, 215-216
    bathrooms, 179-180
    bedrooms, 164
    buyer's vision, 39
    cleaning supplies, 47
    closets, 191-192
    dining rooms, 134
    entryways, 106
    estate homes, 233
    fitness equipment, 42
    fun paraphernalia, 44-46
    furniture, 43
    garages, 47, 219
    hallways, 111
    handling clutter, 50-51
    hiding personal issues, 39
    highlighting features, 38
    home offices, 204-206
    kitchens, 47, 148
        appliances, 149
        countertops, 151

hanging pot racks/tools,
    152
    sinks, 149
    trashcans, 151
living rooms, 120-121
medicines, 44
mementos/gifts, 41
outdoor spaces, 47
personal papers, 40-41
pet, 46
plants, 43
reading material, 42
reducing distractions, 38
rental properties, 232
repair projects, 42
seasonal clothes, 46
spaciousness, 38
stairways, 111
techniques
    focusing, 49
    goal setting, 48
    helpful sayings, 50
    packing, 48
    rewarding yourself, 49
    starting, 48
time saver, 40
toys, 43
vacation homes, 228
decorating magazines, 21
dining rooms, 132
    arranging, 135
    china cabinets, 137
    cleaning, 134
    creating, 140
    decluttering, 134
    Do's, 138
    Don'ts, 138
    furniture, 132
    lighting, 136
    repairs, 133-134
Do's/Don'ts for dining rooms,
    138
doing it yourself staging, 9
doors, 89-91

driveways, 85
drywall installers, 81

E

electrical check-ups, 72
electricians, 81
Electronic Appraiser website,
    12
entryways, 103-106
    budgets, 105
    buyer impressions, 104
    cleaning, 106
    creating, 109
    decluttering, 106
    repairs, 106
    styles, 108-109
    traffic flow, 105
estate homes
    cleaning, 233
    counters, 234
    decluttering, 233
    floors, 233
    generational cycles, 233
    lighting, 234
    paint, 234
    repairs, 234
estate sales, 233
exceptional homes, 227
    estate
        cleaning, 233
        counters, 234
        decluttering, 233
        floors, 233
        generational cycles, 233
        lighting, 234
        paint, 234
        repairs, 234
    estate sales, 233
    flipped houses, 234
    historic homes, 237
    rental properties, 231
        arranging, 232
        audience, 231-232

cleaning, 232
decluttering, 232
research, 231
vacant homes, 235-236
vacation homes, 228
accessories, 229-230
decluttering, 228
renters, 230
spaciousness, 228
exits, 114-115
exterior first impressions
15 second rule, 84
adornments, 94-95
decks, 92
defined, 83
doors, 89-91
driveways, 85
house color, 87-88
house numbers, 93
landscaping, 96-99
lighting, 95
mailboxes, 93
pets, 96
ponds/water fountains, 92
pools, 92
porches, 92
prioritizing, 29
roof, 89
sidewalks, 86-87
trim/accent color, 88-89
welcome mats, 94
exterior photographs, 244

F

family rooms, 118
cleaning, 121
decluttering, 120-121
fireplaces, 118
flooring, 119
floor space, 123
furniture placement,
122-124
lighting, 123-124

painting, 119
styles, 125
decorating tools,
126-127
new decorating
approach, 128
fans in bathrooms, 178
features of rooms, 38
Feng Shui, 206
finished basements, 215
fireplaces, 57, 118
first impressions, 8-9
curb appeal
15 second rule, 84
adornments, 94-95
decks, 92
defined, 83
doors, 89-91
driveways, 85
house color, 87-88
house numbers, 93
landscaping, 96-99
lighting, 95
mailboxes, 93
pets, 96
ponds/water fountains,
92
pools, 92
porches, 92
prioritizing, 29
roof, 89
sidewalks, 86-87
trim/accent color, 88-89
welcome mats, 94
entryways, 103-106
budgets, 105
buyer impressions, 104
cleaning, 106
creating entryways, 109
decluttering, 106
repairs, 106
styles, 108-109
traffic flow, 105
views, 110

fitness equipment, 42
fliers with photographs, 241
flipping houses, 234
floors
bathrooms, 177
bedrooms, 162
cleaning, 57-58
estate homes, 233
kitchens, 75, 147
living rooms, 119
remodeling, 78-79
floor space, 123
floral arrangements, 43
focal points of bedrooms,
158-159
foundations, 73
foyers, 103-106
budgets, 105
buyer impressions, 104
cleaning, 106
creating, 109
decluttering, 106
repairs, 106
styles, 108-109
traffic flow, 105
Freecycle website, 38
Free Home Appraisal website,
12
fun paraphernalia, 44-46
furnace, 71
furniture
bedrooms, 160
cleaning, 57
decluttering, 43
dining rooms, 132
family rooms, 122-124
vacant homes, 235-236
placement
bedrooms, 168-169
dining rooms, 135
home offices, 206-207
living rooms, 122-124

G

garages, 219
  cleaning, 219
  decluttering, 47, 219
  styles, 220
garbage bags for decluttering, 48
gifts, 41
goals
  decluttering, 48
  open houses, 251
grout, 178
guest bedrooms, 173

H

half-baths, 186
half-full closets, 188
hall closets, 197
hallways
  cleaning, 112
  decluttering, 111
  styles, 112
handling clutter, 50-51
hanging pot racks, 152
hardwood floor specialists, 81
heating, ventilation, air conditioning (HVAC) installers, 81
helpful decluttering sayings, 50
hiding personal issues, 39
highlighting room features, 38
historic homes, 237
HomeGain website, 12
HomeInsight website, 12
home offices, 202
  arranging, 206,-207
  cleaning, 204
  closets, 205
  creative spaces, 204
  decluttering, 204-206

  lighting, 206
  purpose, 202
  styles, 208-209
house colors, 87-89
house numbers, 93
HVAC (heating, ventilation, air conditioning) installers, 81

I-J

impressions
  buyers, 8-9
  competitors, 14-15
inspections
  do-it-yourself, 68
  professional inspectors, 67-68
interior first impressions, 103-106
  entryways
    budgets, 105
    buyer impressions, 104
    cleaning, 106
    creating entryways, 109
    decluttering, 106
    repairs, 106
    styles, 108-109
    traffic flow, 105
  views, 110
interior photographs, 243
IRS important papers website, 40

K

kitchens
  appliances, 76, 149
  cabinets, 74
  cleaning, 58-59
  counters, 74
    decluttering/cleaning, 151
    repairing, 145-146

  decluttering, 47, 148
  flooring, 75, 147
  hanging pot racks/tools, 152
  lighting, 148
  pantries, 193
  remodeling, 73-77
  sinks, 77, 149
  stove hoods, 144
  styles, 153-155
  tiles, 144
  trashcans, 151
  walls, 147

L

landscaping
  architects, 81
  curb appeal, 96-99
laundry areas, 222-223
lawn maintenance, 81
lead paint, 69
lifecycles of neighborhoods, 16-17
lighting
  basements, 216-217
  bedrooms, 162, 165-166
  closets, 192
  dining rooms, 136
  estate homes, 234
  home offices, 206
  kitchens, 148
  living rooms, 123-124
  open houses, 248
  outdoors, 95
  photographs, 243
linen closets, 194
living rooms, 118
  cleaning, 121
  decluttering, 120-121
  fireplaces, 118
  flooring, 119
  floor space, 123

furniture placement, 122-124
lighting, 123-124
paint, 119
styles, 125
  decorating tools, 126-127
  new decorating approach, 128
living zones in basements, 217

M

magazines
  decluttering, 42
  decorating, 21
mailboxes, 93
major remodeling, 64
  additions, 79
  basements, 79
  bathrooms, 77-78
  comparing to neighbors, 64-67
  electrical, 72
  floors, 78-79
  foundations, 73
  inspections
    do-it-yourself, 68
    professional inspectors, 67-68
  kitchens, 73-77
  mechanical systems, 70
    electrical, 72
    foundations, 73
    furnace/air conditioning, 71
    plumbing, 72
    roofs, 71
    water heaters, 72
  mold, 69-70
  plumbing, 72
  professionals
    architect, 80-85

bricklayers/stone masons, 80
carpenters, 80
carpet installers, 80
concrete/cement workers, 80
contractors, 80
drywall installers, 81
electricians, 81
hardwood floor specialists, 81
HVAC installers, 81
landscape architects, 81
lawn/yard maintenance, 81
painters, 82
plumbers, 82
roofers, 82
radon, 70
roofs, 71
safety issues
  asbestos, 70
  lead paint, 69
  mold, 69
  radon, 70
  smoke detectors, 69
water heaters, 72
MASP (Master Accredited Staging Professionals), 4
master bedrooms, 161, 196
mechanical system checks, 70
  electrical, 72
  foundations, 73
  furnace/air conditioning, 71
  plumbing, 72
  roofs, 71
  water heaters, 72
medicines, 44
mementos, 41
MLS (multiple listing system), 14, 241
mold, 69

N-O

National Association of Home Inspectors, 68
neighborhoods, 16-17
nontoxic cleaning alternatives, 61

objectivity, 5
odors
  basements, 216
  open house preparations, 247
  pets, 60
  sniff test, 19-20
offices, 202
  arranging, 206-207
  cleaning, 204
  closets, 205
  decluttering, 204-206
  lighting, 206
  purpose, 202
  styles, 208-209
open houses
  advantages, 245
  appointments, 247
  brokers, 246
  disadvantages, 244
  preparing for
    final checklist, 249
    goal, 251
    light, 248
    nature inside, 247-248
    odors, 247
    parking, 250
    pets, 249
    slowing down buyers, 250
    taglines, 251
    valuables, 248
  public, 246
  real estate agent, 246

outside
cleaning, 60-61
decluttering, 47

P–Q

packing, 48
paint
bedrooms, 162
estate homes, 234
house color, 87-88
kitchens, 147
living rooms, 119
trim/accent colors, 88-89
painters, 82
pantries, 193
paper hangers, 82
papers, 40-41
paraphernalia, 44-46
Pareto Principle, (80/20 rule) 38
parking for open houses, 250
personal care products, 44
personal issues, 39
personal papers, 40-41
personal websites, 241
pets
cleaning up after, 60
curb appeal, 96
decluttering, 46
smells, 60
photographs
after staging, 240
agent websites, 241
before staging, 17-19
comprehensive shots, 241
controlling, 242
equipment, 242
fliers, 241
functions, 241
importance, 239
interior, 243
lighting, 243
MLS, 241

personal websites, 241
replicating exactly as
before pictures, 240
seasonal decorations, 244
tips for better pictures
exterior, 244
focusing on the room,
243
seasonal decorations,
244
pillows, 127
plants, 43
play equipment, 98
plumbers, 82
plumbing, 72
ponds, 92
pools, 92
porcelain tiles, 75
porches, 92
powder rooms, 186
power washers, 60
preferences of buyers, 4
preparing for open houses
final checklist, 249
goal, 251
light, 248
nature inside, 247-248
odors, 247
parking, 250
pets, 249
slowing down buyers, 250
taglines, 251
valuables, 248
price points, 12
amenities, 13-14
appraisals, 12-13
competitor impressions,
14-15
prioritizing rooms, 29-31
professionals for remodeling
architects, 80, 85
bricklayers/stone masons,
80
carpenters, 80

carpet installers, 80
concrete/cement workers,
80
contractors, 80
drywall installers, 81
electricians, 81
hardwood floor specialists,
81
HVAC installers, 81
landscape architects, 81
lawn/yard maintenance, 81
painters, 82
plumbers, 82
roofers, 82
public open houses, 246. *See
also* open houses

R

radon, 70
reading material, 42
real estate agent open houses,
246
Realtor.com website, 12
redundant furniture, 43
refacing cabinets, 74
remodeling, 64. *See also*
repairs
additions, 79
basements, 79
bathrooms, 77-78
comparing to neighbors,
64-67
electrical, 72
floors, 78-79
foundations, 73
inspections, 67-68
kitchens, 73-77
lead paint, 69
mechanical systems, 70-71
electrical, 72
foundations, 73
furnace/air condition-
ing, 71

plumbing, 72
roofs, 71
water heaters, 72
mold, 69-70
plumbing, 72
professionals
architects, 80, 85
bricklayers/stone
masons, 80
carpenters, 80
carpet installers, 80
concrete/cement
workers, 80
contractors, 80
drywall installers, 81
electricians, 81
hardwood floor
specialists, 81
HVAC installers, 81
landscape architects, 81
lawn/yard maintenance,
81
painters, 82
plumbers, 82
roofers, 82
radon, 70
roofs, 71
safety issues, 69
water heaters, 72
rental properties, 231
arranging, 232
audience, 231-232
cleaning, 232
decluttering, 232
research, 231
renters, 230
repairs, 42. *See also* remodeling
bathrooms
counters, 177
fans, 178
floors, 177
grout/caulking, 178
walls, 176
bedrooms, 162

closets, 190
dining rooms, 133-134
entryways, 106
estate homes, 234
kitchens
countertops, 145-146
flooring, 147
lighting, 148
stove hoods, 144
tiles, 144
walls, 147
researching
homes, 15
impressions, 14-15
neighborhood lifecycles,
16-17
standards, 16
rental properties, 231
styles, 20-22
return ratio of staging, 8
rewarding yourself, 49
roofers, 82
roofs, 71, 89
rooms
distractions, 38
highlighting features, 38
prioritizing, 29-31
RVs, 220

S

safety issues
asbestos, 70
lead paint, 69
mold, 69
radon, 70
smoke detectors, 69
saving time decluttering, 40
seasonal clothing, 46
seasonal decorations, 244
secondary bedrooms, 161
sidewalks, 86-87
sight lines, 122
sinks, 77, 149

smells, 19-20
basements, 216
open house preparations,
247
pets, 60
sniff test, 19-20
smoke detectors, 69
sniff test, 19-20
spaciousness
basements, 216-217
bathrooms, 181-182
bedrooms, 166
closets, 198-199
decluttering, 38
vacation homes, 228
spa image of bathrooms,
182-184
staging
benefits, 6-7
buyer preferences, aid-
ing, 4
competitive advantages,
4
objectivity, 5
defined, 4
return ratio, 8
statistics, 7-8
stairways
cleaning, 112
decluttering, 111
styles, 112
standards for home comparisons, 16
starting decluttering, 48
statistics, 7-8
stone masons, 80
stove hoods, 144
styles
basements, 218-219
bedrooms, 170
entryways, 108-109
garages, 220
hallways, 112
home offices, 208-209

kitchens, 153-155
living rooms, 125
    decorating tools,
        126-127
    new decorating
        approach, 128
on trend, 20-22
researching, 20-22
stairways, 112

T

taglines, 251
techniques for decluttering
    focusing, 49
    goal setting, 48
    helpful sayings, 50
    packing, 48
    rewarding yourself, 49
    starting, 48
tiles, 144
tips for better photographs
    equipment, 242
    exterior, 244
    focusing on the room, 243
    lighting, 243
toilets, 78
toilet seats, 59
toys, 43
trashcans, 151
trees, 98
on trend, 20-22
trim colors, 88-89
tubs, 78

U-V

unfinished basements, 214
up-side potential, 26

vacant homes, 235-236
vacation homes, 228
    accessories, 229-230
    decluttering, 228

renters, 230
    spaciousness, 228
ValueMyHouse website, 12
value of homes, 12
    amenities, 13-14
    appraisals, 12-13
    competitor impressions,
        14-15
views of rooms, 110
vignettes, 127

W-X-Y-Z

wallpaper borders, 140
walls
    bathrooms, 176
    cleaning, 56-57
    kitchens, 147
    wallpaper borders, 140
water fountains, 92
water heaters, 72
websites
    appraisals, 12
    Century 21, 14
    Coldwell Banker, 14
    Electronic Appraiser, 12
    Freecycle, 38
    Free Home Appraisal, 12
    HomeGain, 12
    HomeInsight, 12
    IRS important papers, 40
    Realtor.com, 12
    ValueMyHouse, 12
welcome mats, 94
windows, 55
woodwork, 56

yard maintenance, 81

Check Out These Best-Sellers